THE CHRISTIAN OUTSIDER

The Epworth Press is happy to publish what follows as a vivid contribution to the debate about the future of 'the Christian presence' in human society. It by no means endorses all the author's opinions.

Ray Billington

THE CHRISTIAN OUTSIDER

London EPWORTH PRESS

CONTENTS

ACKNOWLEDGEMENTS

The author and publishers are grateful for permission to quote from the following: *The New Creation as Metropolis*, by G. Winter, Collier-Macmillan Limited; *The Noise of Solemn Assemblies*, by Peter L. Berger, Doubleday & Company, Inc.; *Free to Live, Free to Die*, by Malcolm Boyd, Holt, Rinehart and Winston Inc.; *Objections to Humanism*, by Ronald Hepburn, Constable and Prof. Ronald Hepburn; *The Secular Meaning of the Gospel*, by Paul Van Buren, *The Secular City*, by Harvey Cox, *On Not Leaving it to the Snake*, by Harvey Cox, S.C.M. Press Ltd; *Do We Need the Church?* by Richard McBrien, Collins Publishers; *Introduction to Moral Education*, by Norman Williams, *Has Man a Future?* by Bertrand Russell, Penguin Books Ltd; *Rain Upon Godshill*, by J. B. Priestley, William Heinemann Ltd, Publishers.

It is idle to curse the human condition. It is stupid to be alienated from everyone and also from oneself. The exit is to begin – one must begin for oneself, with no one else to say why or how; one must lift oneself by one's own bootstraps, in an act of gratuitous, creative freedom; one must create oneself out of nothingness. The exit is to begin to experience, to understand, to judge, to decide. For such acts, more than any others, enlarge the range of one's self and of one's world. One must begin (with a little help from one's friends) to feel, to intuit, to evaluate, to do.

The revolution is in the human spirit or not at all.

– Michael Novak
A Theology for Radical Politics

FOREWORD

THE SECTION headings of this book make its theme, or themes, self-explanatory. Beginning in 1964, when I first joined the staff of St. Mary's, Woolwich, I follow through, as systematically as possible, the development of my ideas during the subsequent six years. If there is, therefore, an element of self-contradiction occasionally, the reader will appreciate that the convictions of yesterday can become the doubts of today and the disbeliefs of tomorrow; or vice versa.

If the occasional autobiographical note is irksome, I apologize. The development of thinking recorded in the book seemed to demand some personal background information from time to time; on reflection, it seems that there is a closer link between ideas held and decisions taken than was always evident at the time. As I say in the postscript, man is indivisible: but this applies not only to the race as a whole but also to man as a single entity. Thought and action, the mental and the physical, are interrelated, and it is sometimes difficult to state which is cause and which effect.

There is a marked contrast in outlook and style with my previous book, *The Liturgical Movement and Methodism*. I stated in the preface to that volume that one must write according to one's readership: there I had church members chiefly in mind; here it is anticipated that, while those who remain church-affiliated will wish to consider what I have to say, my thesis will be more acceptable to those with no such affiliation. This is not another book analysing what's wrong with the Church, but one born out of concern for the human situation, and the conviction that this can be dealt with only on human terms, with human knowledge, insight, and compassion. Those who prefer to face the world from a religious context will probably find that the earlier thesis speaks more than this one does to their condition.

Insofar as this book reflects a change of direction on my part since writing about the Liturgical Movement, it may be argued that it invalidates what was written earlier. My view is, however, that a man's life and work must be taken as a whole; some people will be sympathetic to one aspect, others to another. I am told that there are still pacifists who find my small book *The Basis of*

Pacifist Conviction helpful: yet I am myself no longer a pacifist. Does it matter that I have replaced earlier ideas if people still find these helpful in their particular situation? I met last year a woman now in her forties who informed me that an evangelical appeal that I had made twenty years ago, to which she had responded by 'coming forward', had changed her life. The fact that I quickly rejected this method of conducting services, and am now wholly antipathetic to it, cannot discount the good that was clearly done at that moment.

If Brecht is right, that we are what we have done, then most of us are a pretty illogical rag-bag. Even if I am more illogical than most when the total spectrum of life is seen as a panorama, it is a difference more of degree than of kind.

My indebtedness to various writers will be apparent throughout the book, but I must mention especially the many correspondents who have shared their thinking with me over the years covered in the four sections. There has been space for only a few of their letters; ten times as many deserve to be quoted.

I conclude with a word of tribute to my wife. My friends assure me that to have married me would be enough to shatter the faith of most women. Whether my wife's Roman Catholic upbringing helped her to stand firm, I cannot tell; nor am I certain how far she relishes being an epitomized ecumenical movement, moving first to Methodism, then, at St. Mary's, to Anglicanism, through non-church to whatever she is now. Perhaps it is as well that, while we view life retrospectively, we live it prospectively; if it had been the other way round, who knows what she might have said when asked the somewhat pointed question at the altar? As it is, I know that the writing of this book has been eased by her sympathy (meaning, I suspect, consent rather than assent), and I hope that not too many will condemn her on that account.

Bristol, 1970   RAY BILLINGTON

Section One

WOOLWICH

I JOINED the staff of St. Mary's Church, Woolwich, in September 1964. If what follows is critical of Woolwich, it must not be thought that I am ungrateful for its opportunities or unmindful of the rector's, Nicolas Stacey's, kindness in many ways.

Immediately the glare of the mass media was turned in my direction. The rector believed firmly that these media of communication, the new fact of life in the twentieth century, existed to be used. Consequently, it was the Church's responsibility to make use of them whenever the occasion deserved it, rather than leave the field wide open to divorcees, juvenile thugs, or film starlets who would drop anything at a cameraman's nod. Inevitably, the pendulum swung too far in our direction, and by the end of the four years of the 'Woolwich experiment' (a neutral enough title to claim, since not all experiments are successful) we were suffering from over-exposure. Since the natural tendency of the mass media is to sensationalize (by which I mean that, if given the choice, those responsible will spotlight what they consider will be of widest interest, rather than what is ultimately most important) there was also the added danger of distortion.

The background

What, then, actually happened at Woolwich, and what is its significance, if any? Having had two years away from it all, I feel it possible to offer an objective, if still somewhat personal, account. The fact that – as this book will progressively indicate – my own views about the Church and theology have changed since my time in Woolwich will not, it is hoped, lessen the value of the assessment. Since it was my experiences there which, more than anything else, caused my change of direction, it seems not unimportant to analyse these.

The facts of the four years can be outlined chronologically. When I joined the staff, it consisted of the rector and four curates – Richard Garrard, Brian Cooper, Jeffrey Rowthorne and Jeremy

Hurst. All were Anglican, energetic, and young, with a public school and/or university background. During the previous two to three years, they – or those whom they had replaced (Paul Bibby and Bob Hughes) – had worked as a fairly conventional, though obviously larger-than-usual, Anglican staff. It is important that this be understood, since the newspaper article which first widely publicized St. Mary's – Stacey's *Observer* colour supplement article in December 1964 – was frequently quoted against us in later years as a confession of failure in all that followed. It was not. That article simply stated that after virtually three years of intense parochial work by four or five clergymen, Woolwich remained unimpressed, and congregations much the same as under the previous incumbency. The article's conclusion was that the *traditional* methods of building up congregations were no longer viable; but this conclusion was blurred by the article's title – 'Woolwich – a Mission's Failure' – which seemed to imply that non-traditional methods were also doomed. I now believe this to be the case, but at the time this was virgin territory which had to be explored.

My arrival gave the other members of the staff the opportunity to begin a change of direction. I was earning nothing from the church, but had three part-time jobs lined up: editing *Over the Bridge*, magazine of the South London Industrial Mission; teaching at the Woolwich Polytechnic Secondary School; and lecturing at the Woolwich College for Further Education, to which I went full-time after two years. Jeremy Hurst was the first to take a similar step, accepting a post at a local comprehensive school early in 1965. Before this, we had been joined by Barbara Wollestan, a trained sociologist, who began by undertaking a study of the congregation and its needs, and then became one of the officials at the planning stage of the new town of Thamesmead, further down the river. The concept of having on a church staff men and women who presented no financial liability to the church was not new, but at St. Mary's this practice grew beyond anything seen elsewhere. We were joined by Peggy Taylor, the headmistress of the local Church primary school, by Richard Christian, an Anglican priest teaching in a secondary modern school, and by several others on a similar basis who remained for shorter periods.

In March 1965 the Presbyterian Church in Woolwich closed down and, following negotiations which had lasted nearly two years, the congregation moved to St. Mary's, which was renamed 'St. Mary's with St. Andrew's'. The two congregations worshipped separately on Sunday mornings, unitedly in the evenings, the form of this service varying from week to week. The Parochial Church Council of St. Mary's, and the Presbyterian Session of St. Andrew's, continued to function, the intention being that the two bodies should not immediately abandon autonomy, but should grow together naturally. The Presbyterian minister, Derek Baker, joined the staff; and he was joined a few months later by Paul Jobson, who replaced Jeffrey Rowthorne, and after a year became full-time youth leader with the bulk of his salary paid by the local Authority.

Three other appointments should be mentioned in this somewhat bald summary: in 1966 Richard Garrard, who had by then been made 'sub-rector' (a post which does not legally exist in the Anglican Church, but this seemed an unimportant consideration since Richard was chief pastor to the Anglican congregation) was replaced by Michael Covington; and during the following year a Baptist minister, Brian Challis, joined us as chief administrator of the Quadrant Housing Association, which Stacey had founded and at that time operated from the St. Mary's offices. Finally, we were joined by a Belgian Benedictine priest, Henri de Halgouet, who earned his living by teaching at a local girls' comprehensive school.

During my first two years, the staff met daily for Mattins and Evensong, to which, of course, the congregation were invited. There were weekly staff meetings on Monday mornings which, under Stacey's chairmanship, were remarkably businesslike; no time was allowed for idle reminiscences or speculation, and each of us had the opportunity to raise for discussion issues concerning our own areas of work which might relate to the church's activities in general and the team's in particular. On Sundays we shared in leading the services, the chief discipline here for me being that of reducing my usual 25-minute sermons in Methodist churches to seven minutes at the morning Eucharist and 15 minutes in the evening. In the second two years, when there was a clear-cut distinction between those on the staff who functioned mainly within the church structure, and those who worked outside this, the former carried a somewhat greater share of the responsibilities in the public worship. In this later period, those working in what were then popularly known as the 'secular structures' were not expected to attend Mattins or Evensong; and a full staff meeting was held only fortnightly in the evening, preceded by a brief Communion service held in the Presbyterian vestry, which had been added at the time of the union.

Church activities were kept to a minimum, a women's meeting being the only regular activity apart from the youth work, which was in any case an entity separate from the church, only meeting on the premises. We did not encourage people to become confirmed, and I doubt if more than twenty were so received into the church during my period there. We held occasional short-term teaching courses or house groups in which all the team participated, together with even more occasional day- or weekend conferences. We considered that, in general, the members of the congregation worked hard enough earning their daily bread without feeling under an obligation to trail out again in the evening for what became, in most cases that we had experienced, idle discussion, in the sense that talk revolved around what 'ought' to be and not what could and would be done.

Attendances at the Sunday services remained steady during my four years: around 70 at the morning Eucharist, 50 at the Presbyterian service, and 90 in the evening. Obviously, the occasional 'special' saw better attendances, which suggested to some of us on the staff that we should have been wiser to rationalize the situation and hold only three or four services a year, together with the odd weekend conference. It seems demonstrable that most people who attend church at all prefer the services to partake of the element of an 'occasion' – and this cannot be every week. We were not unduly distressed (or if anyone was, he kept it to himself) about the evident disinterest in our church activities displayed by the people of Woolwich; our concern was the daily contacts of the team and congregation, and the invitation to 'come to church' was one that I, and others there, had ceased to make. Few things, we felt, would be more likely to distract a person who was beginning to reflect on basic values more than having to sit through a church service. We were consequently unimpressed by the cuttings, which reached us through the post from time to time, outlining how vigorous and active some churches were, with rooms packed every night with people seeking 'fellowship'.

I hope this does not sound either condescending or cynical. The fact is that the concern of most members of the team was with the area in which each worked from Mondays to Fridays. Whatever it was that we possessed as Christians had to be expressed and tested primarily in that sphere, and our hope was that our existence as a team would give each of us a focal point, and a source of joy, in what we were doing. Put in theological terms, we were concerned more about the Kingdom of God than about the Church.

However, as the team expanded the question of where our loyalty lay – to the team or to the church congregation – became increasingly a cause of tension. Without any form of pastoral oversight, and having few opportunities to lead the congregation in worship, some members inevitably felt that the team was primary, the congregation secondary. Indeed, it was the publicity given to the team rather than to the church which attracted some of its members from the start; and the occasional half-hearted attempts to 'involve' all the members in some congregational activity seem in retrospect to have been artificial. The fact of the matter is that by the end of 1967 only two members – Michael Covington among the Anglicans and Derek Baker among the Presbyterians – were in close touch with the congregation. Nick Stacey was 'around', in the sense that he had an office on the premises; but he was engaged more in writing than in pastoralia. Paul Jobson conducted his youth activities full-time from an office in the crypt, but most of this work was independent of other congregational activities. The rest of us were seen by church members only on Sundays, and many of these members were considerably more regular in attendance than we were.

On reflection, it seems that we had created a unit which was largely independent of any established body of people. The church's existence; its need for a rector; the arrival of Stacey in this post: all these combined to spawn what eventually became a small group of like-minded people. But, like any offspring, the time came when we, or some of us, required increasing self-determination. There were team members who regretted this, in the conviction that our *raison d'être* was the church and its congregation. To me this view was unacceptable. I had some good friends in the congregation, and some of them had a fairly clear understanding of what the team was trying to achieve. Yet there was always a gap between the concepts and practices of most of the team and those of the congregation; and this gap widened with time. Were we to stop thinking, cease experimentation, until the larger body had 'caught up' with us? (Conversely, if what we were doing was ill-advised, were we to wait until we had dragged the congregation down to our level?)

This issue was one of the chief factors which led me to think and write along the lines of what I termed 'non-church', which I shall discuss in the next section. It was, therefore, a matter of some regret to me that during my final year at St. Mary's the policy adopted was that of not taking the congregation too rapidly beyond what it could 'take'. Since it had never been asked to take anything particularly exciting, with the exception of the occasional experimental services (using drama, guitars, and dialogue sermons) this might have seemed to an outside observer, as it did to me, a platitudinous statement. Not so: following a questionnaire to all the members, in which they were asked to state their liturgical preferences, most of the minor permanent changes in worship were abolished. The choir, who had been persuaded to sit where they belonged with the congregation, where they could be heard but not seen – returned to their stalls where they could be seen but not heard. We had adopted the new Anglican liturgy of the Eucharist, the chief advantage of which, compared with 1662, was its brevity, but the optional sections of this which we had originally omitted – including the *Gloria in Excelsis* and the Prayer of Humble Access – were restored.

These matters, of course, were not in themselves important enough to cause more than momentary vexation. Yet to some of us, particularly Paul Jobson and myself, they symbolized and epitomized a radical difference of outlook between staff and congregation which brought home the truth about the new wine in the old skins. It was not that the congregation was wrong in deciding as it did: our disquiet arose from the difference of perspective between us which these and other similar decisions exposed.

Although, therefore, Stacey's translation to Oxfam in April 1968 hastened the departure of some members of the team, my own decision to leave had been made some months before this. Had we been able to re-group ourselves independently altogether of the church, this decision might have been different. But since the team had from its inception been closely linked with the congregation, and since not all, or even the majority, were desirous, like me, of breaking any link with an existing congregation, there was no real choice on the matter. Such a re-grafting would, in any case, have raised the problem of the old skins and new wine which, as I have said, had already caused considerable frustration.

So, in the summer of 1968, the dispersion took place, and two years later only three of the team remain. The appointment of Stacey's successor ensured, rightly or wrongly, that the more adventurous aspects of the experiment would cease, and the church has returned to its status before it began – that of a run-of-the-mill Anglican church, with the one exception that the Presbyterian congregation and minister remain in the shared building. Whether the values that the team was seeking to explore and express continue to motivate the members in their new spheres, I cannot tell; we have no reunions, and any meetings between us are accidental. Certainly whatever of worth we embodied as a team has disappeared; and the issue which we must now examine is whether the Woolwich experiment has made any lasting contribution to the Church, to Christian teaching, or to human values generally.

Assessment of the Experiment

There are four areas which I shall outline under this heading where the team in its decisions and activities subserved either the Church in particular or the human situation in general. Before considering these, let me briefly outline the areas of weakness in the set-up – briefly, because they were palpable to anyone who knew the team and its activities well.

From the start, the team was always too much influenced and controlled by the strongest personality, Stacey. In this it contrasted strongly with the Methodist Group ministry in Notting Hill. There, the status of each member was the same; each had his contribution to make; and none was accepted as pre-eminent. In Woolwich it was impossible to escape from the rector/curate syndrome; consequently, the Anglican members tended always to be subservient to Stacey. Officially, of course, all decisions were team decisions, and Stacey could be outvoted on any issue. In fact I suspect that the only issues on which he allowed this latter state of affairs to operate were those on which he did not feel strongly anyway.

The Free Church members of the team were not so beholden to the rector as were the Anglicans; but, because he was the founder and chairman of the team, we were all of us inevitably affected by his outlook. This was most evident during the final year, when he had clearly become bored with the whole project and was looking for more fertile pastures for his particular brand of dynamism. This growing indifference was reflected in the team, and the last year lacked the sense of cohesion evinced in the earlier years. Each member tended to become increasingly involved in his own particular activities, and, as I have indicated, a rift occurred between us on the question of contacts with the congregation.

Differences of opinion and occasional heated arguments between any group of twelve or so people working together are hardly likely to be avoided, as any study of the Gospels will demonstrate; but these can be borne provided general agreement remains about the direction to be taken. During that final year it became apparent that the team were divided on this central issue, and I doubt if we could have continued without splitting into two groups – those whose activities centred chiefly on the church, motivated primarily by its renewal or reformation; and those who looked to the so-called secular structures as their base, and were looking for revolution rather than renewal in the Church.

Perhaps the later occupations of the team members indicate where their main interests lay: Stacey a deputy director of Oxfam; Rowthorne lecturing in theology in the United States; Hugh as Student Welfare Officer at Birmingham University; Cooper as Vice-Principal of a theological college; Garrard and Jobson as chaplains to colleges of education; Hurst as Head of Modern Languages in a comprehensive school; Covington as a curate in the Midlands; Barbara Wollestan as a sociologist with the GLC; Peggy Taylor as a headmistress; Christian as another educational college chaplain; Baker remains Presbyterian minister at St. Mary's; Challis is minister of a Baptist church; I lecture in Liberal Studies in a Polytechnic; and Fr. Henri, in many ways the most visionary of us all, continues his quest in Canada. Perhaps the academic qualifications represented on the staff were more of a hindrance than a help in communicating with the people of Woolwich.

I shall now outline the insights offered by the experiment, in what I consider to be ascending order of importance. In each case I shall add my own present thoughts on the matter, which are not necessarily (and probably not at all) those of other team members.

1. Use of church buildings

This was an aspect of the work which was well publicized, but it may be helpful to summarize what happened.

Before I arrived, the gallery had been converted into a restaurant and coffee bar on one side, and a lounge on the other. The restaurant was sub-let to a manager, who paid a rent to the church and was responsible for its economic viability. About fifty lunches were served daily to local business people, and it was used by the church for such activities as post-communion breakfast each week. The lounge was necessary, since there was literally

Wegzeichen; Festgabe zum 60. Geburtstag von Hermenegild M. Biedermann. Hrsg. von Ernst Chr. Suttner und C. Patock.

Würzburg   Augustinus-Verlag

1971

(Das Östliche Christentum, n.F., Heft 25)

Dottie Cross

no other room on the premises where such meetings as those of the PCC could be held.

As mentioned, two Presbyterian vestries were added at the time of the union. In 1966, the side aisles, which were rarely required in the services, were converted into sets of offices, three on each side, which were rented to the local Council and used for the Social Welfare department. Apart from the financial benefits accruing to the church from this move, the remaining body of the building, being more compact, was psychologically more suited to congregational participation, as looked for in many expressions of the Liturgical Movement. The Council, for their part, gained some much-needed extra space; and the choice of the welfare and social services was extremely felicitous, since the church was removed from the centre of the borough, in pleasant gardens overlooking the Thames, and those making use of the services felt less exposed than was inevitable in a centrally-sited public building like a town hall.

The speed of operation here was remarkable. The time between the idea occurring to Nick on a train from Charing Cross to Woolwich, including discussion by the staff and the PCC, the drawing up of plans by the borough architect, and the work being set into motion, was a matter of days rather than weeks. When I reflect on the profusion of multiloquous verbosity required in most churches before a roof can be repaired or a pulpit redesigned, I marvel at the obstacle-free progress of this change. Almost as an after-thought we decided at the same time to remove the pews (my proposal to sell them as religious relics was not taken seriously, though some were, incredibly enough, bought by other churches) and replace them with stackable chairs which were given added stability for kneelers by the laying of a carpet over the entire nave.

The final change was the one which caused most furore outside, especially in Free Church circles. The crypt, which I imagine had not previously been used, except at his peril, by anyone over the height of four feet, was dug out and converted into a ritzy discothèque and bar. It was used on five nights of the week for various youth activities; and what caused us to be condemned in some quarters as disciples of Bacchus was the licensing of the bar on Tuesday and Thursday evenings for folk-singing and jazz with the over-eighteens. I argued at the time in the *Methodist Recorder* that there was no question that those who joined in would not be drinking somewhere on these evenings, so that not to have secured a licence would have excluded us from communication with this age group. The refusal of total abstainers to recognize this, and their stated preference for no dealings with the people concerned rather than dealings over a quiet drink, exemplified to my mind the stagnancy of absolutist ethical thinking. I return to this in the final section when discussing the basis of morality.

This left only the chancel and the central nave of the church unaltered in shape. It was mooted at one time that since the chancel was lifted above the nave, and consisted of various expressions of interesting stonework, it was ideally suited for dramatic productions. Other cultural activities such as musical concerts could easily be accommodated there. Both of these did occasionally take place, but there was a certain hesitancy about this in the minds of many, deriving from the concept of the holy place, the sanctuary. Gordon Davies has shown, in his *Secular Use of Church Buildings* (SCM), how in the Middle Ages the chancel and nave were used throughout the week in most churches for the so-called secular activities of the local community. Our unwillingness to take this step, which could have been achieved simply by letting it be known locally that the building was available for meetings of various types, was regrettable.

Our experience in this field leads me to two conclusions, both admittedly incompatible. Firstly, if congregations of the future wish to maintain their private buildings, then on financial and possibly theological grounds this seems the wisest use for them. Income is assured (and many buildings are sited in highly desirable areas of boroughs) and space, which in many cities is at a premium, is not wasted. With a little imagination and initiative, together with the personal assurance about the policy's merits which is strong enough to withstand opposition and perhaps animosity, many other buildings could at the same time be rid of the burden of maintenance and provide a service to the local community. Anyone acquainted with the Methodist Central Halls will understand this.

The second conclusion goes further. It is that church buildings of any kind are an intolerable burden for any congregation to have to maintain. The appeals for large sums of money for renovations which are continually made by large numbers of churches makes a mockery of several facets of the Gospel which they presumably proclaim. Their very existence militates against the call to 'go out' which lies at the heart of all Christian mission. So long as church buildings exist, they will encourage a sizeable proportion of their congregations to imagine that their responsibilities as

Christians have been fulfilled by spending an hour a week within their walls. Of course, if the view is taken that there are certain places which have been uniquely hallowed, this attitude will not be considered scandalous. The theology underlying this will be considered in later sections. At this point I will simply express my conviction that the treatment of any piece of ground as inherently holier than any other cannot be justified from what we read in the Gospels of the beliefs accepted by Jesus. In the past 'the scandal of the particular' was acknowledged, but considered essential in an imperfect world, whether it was referring to clergymen, buildings, or communion elements. We have now outgrown that concept; and insofar as one of the supreme human needs of our time is to encourage each individual person to be responsible for himself, any doctrine which encourages the acceptance of specially holy people, places or meals must be condemned as a stumbling-block to human progress.

The attachment which some church members have to their building can only be described as frightening. Any minister who has attempted to close a redundant building will have encountered this devotion. Opponents of the closure will appear almost between the floorboards and paving stones in order to prevent the elimination of the ground trodden by their forefathers: laudable as human sentiments, perhaps, but hardly related to the Gospel which gave the building its *raison d'être*.

Is there any need at all to possess private buildings for worship? It is convenient not to have to make special arrangements every week, but is it justified, especially in the light of the declining attendances at services? Can the Church maintain its integrity and still express the worship of Mammon in this way? (For is it not a worship of Mammon to desire the possession of one's own property?)

My view is that the Gospel instructs, and the requirement of a healthy outlook in the Church demands, that these buildings be sold and the money accruing given to the needy. The argument against this action is frequently made by apologists for Anglican income from investments: that such a course is in the category of 'one-off', whereas by maintaining buildings and income the value to the community and the world will continue indefinitely. This begs the enormous question of whether they are of any value in these spheres. Most of the income is spent in maintaining the buildings and their attached personnel; and most of the buildings are used for self-generating purposes. And just as increased possessions bring increased worries, so the more established these buildings are, the more the people who congregate them are compelled to spend time, energy and money on their upkeep. Thus they are inevitably diverted from the human tragedies around them – poverty, loneliness, shallowness of life – and virtues which any average congregation possesses in abundance – compassion, sympathy, dedication, breadth of spirit – are stultified. Throughout ten years in the full-time ministry of the church, I found that the only issue which was *guaranteed* to start people talking and get them working concerned the requirements of the building.

Where, then, would congregations worship? Assuming that in the next generation there will be no more than tiny groups wishing to do so (and all the signs are that worship is a human function representative of man at a stage of his evolution which is now being left behind) it seems reasonable, logical, and fully in accordance with New Testament teaching that this be conducted in a room or building borrowed or hired for the occasion. Other organizations, such as political parties, trade unions, women's institutes, and so on, take it for granted that for their public meetings they will normally hire a room in a school, town hall, or community centre. I cannot see why those who wish to worship regularly should not do the same. All the haggling over buildings, which can stultify the physical, mental and spiritual energies of a congregation, would be obviated in one move: and members would be left free to pursue those creative social activities relating to the needs of the community which, while at the moment not entirely neglected by the Church, are inexorably forced low down on the list of priorities.

One objection to this policy was expressed by Alison Adcock in an article in *New Christian* (14.7.1966). Considering the tensions faced by many city dwellers today, she wrote:

> This man is never, never alone and still in silence. But he can be, in a church, on weekdays, alone, on tiptoe, drinking up stillness and timelessness while the nerves cool and untwist and the perspectives of living swing back into focus. . . . To destroy the last oases of truth and silence in our cities so as to belong more completely to our own age (more secular in the literal sense of less eternal) may merely mean that we destroy our last bridge to sanity and give ourselves over entirely to bedlam, because not many people have the sense to come up for air.

It is a valid point to make that modern man, like his ancestors, continually requires stillness and space. It is not a valid point to make that church buildings are actually used for this purpose by more than a tiny minority of the population, and that this therefore justifies their remaining there, with all the accompanying disadvantages already outlined. Rather it is a challenge to those who plan towns and cities to ensure that the needs of those who occupy the areas are not sacrificed to the builders' profit balances. If the need as outlined by Miss Adcock exists – and I would accept that it does – then the closure of church buildings would compel councils and planners to act in creating answers to this need. So long as the churches are there, planners are able with a relatively easy conscience (insofar as any planner today can have one) to unburden themselves of this responsibility.

To return to the central issue: my basic reason for wishing to see church buildings abandoned is that their existence inevitably creates a system of values which is sub-christian, if not anti-christian. Care of the building replaces care of the community; the invitation to come in replaces the New Testament call to go out; and, as the old hymn expresses it, 'The heathen in his blindness bows down to wood and stone'. I am not claiming that at St. Mary's we had avoided this error: but the steps we were taking were in the right direction, and I'm sure that as time passed we should have proceeded further. In the end, the question of values is unanswerable: one cannot proclaim a Gospel of sacrifice, or argue that all that matters is what a man is, rather than what he has, and at the same time declare of the building: 'Our ancestors built it, our fathers maintained it and we shall preserve it.' This is misplaced loyalty, and the time is long overdue for church congregations to become aware of this, and act upon it.

2. *Ecumenism*

I have already indicated that the areas in which St. Mary's was ecumenical were in the shared use of buildings, and a staff consisting of men from different denominations. Neither of these will startle many people today, but in the second aspect at least we were pioneers. I shall discuss each in turn, and then suggest what I think the experiment indicates about the Church in the immediate future.

(a) *Shared buildings*

The Anglican-Presbyterian experiment challenged the doctrine held in certain quarters that unity is impossible until theological agreement has been reached. If this were taken absolutely literally, we should be compelled to hold half-a-dozen different communion services in the Methodist Church alone, according to the variety of interpretations of what is happening. Fortunately the two churches concerned did not wait for this far-off divine event, but went ahead on the basis of goodwill (for which, again, there seems more Gospel authority than for the theological niceties of eucharistic dogma). There was no case of blood rushing to the head: many meetings were held between the PCC and Session before the initial step was taken; and thereafter every move was carefully discussed by these bodies. The Presbyterians were naturally anxious to preserve a fair degree of autonomy, and Derek Baker was cautious (in my opinion ultra cautious) not to take any step which would offend his people, or to do anything personally that they could not do as a body. (For this reason, he, along with Father Henri, did not communicate when the staff Eucharist was Anglican in form.) Occasional united communion services were held between the two congregations, but in the main they remained separated for their high liturgical events. The evening service, which was a mixture of a variety of liturgical traditions, was the occasion when the two congregations regularly met: at first there was a certain shyness between them, but this was beginning to break down by the time I left. For major decisions affecting both groups, such as the building of the two sets of offices in the side aisles, there were joint meetings of the PCC and Session.

In other words, these congregations were faithfully attempting to put into practice the British Council of Churches' recommendation to congregations not to do anything separately that they could do together. The advantage which we had at Woolwich was that the two congregations could not, because of the physical facts of the situation, avoid each other; and so long as congregations continue to possess their separate buildings, this is precisely what most of them will do for at least as long as Ian Smith in Rhodesia foresees segregation of whites and blacks. So long as you always have your own base to retire to, the occasional forays into the other camp, such as during the Week of Prayer for Christian Unity, will be as unreal in terms of genuine unity as the claims of a schoolchild to be able to swim without ever leaving the side of the baths. (In some ways, the services during the Week of Prayer are proving a hindrance to progress in this direction, since they give congregations the feeling that they've 'done their unity thing' for another twelve months.)

The fact is that if Christians belong together, then they need each other; and if the ingrained habits of the various denominal

22

tions are a deterrent to unity, they must be dropped. Those who want to wait until we've all discovered 'the truth' are crying for the moon. There will be no sign in this generation, any more than there was for Jonah or the Pharisees. I am bound to add that, in my experience, those who talk in grandiose terms about 'truth' and the need for all to discover it invariably mean the theological convictions which they happen to hold themselves. This is the case not only for those who frenziedly wave the Bible (AV) in discussion, but also for those who speak loftily of the 'Tradition' of the Church.

What the ecumenists are up against, of course, is the fact that for many church people their denomination is their club, with its own distinctive rules of membership, its in-talk and in-jokes. ('Heard the one about the circuit steward? . . .' 'There was this curate at his first confession . . .') These people fear that unity will bring about the same defects as amalgamations in industry and comprehensive schools in education: a lessening of the personal element, of a sense of belonging to a family, a close-knit community. People, they feel, will find the odds lengthening on their meeting others at their Church holiday home who know their minister; national conferences will be conferences instead of reunions.

The answer to this is that larger groupings will require more communication locally. Those in the south-east will probably know less than at present about what those in the north-west are doing. This would be a slight loss, but in view of the fact that their chief concern should be with what is happening in the south-east anyway, the gain would outweigh the loss. It would also outweigh the loss, supposing this were to happen, of international contacts within a particular denomination. It is easy enough for Methodists, for instance, to claim brotherhood with fellow Methodists throughout the world. Most of these are thousands of miles away, and out of sight. It is much more difficult, and more important, to be in harmony with local Anglicans. Congregationalists, Presbyterians or Catholics than with brother Methodists in Tennessee, Toronto, or Tonga.

It was a cause of disappointment to us at Woolwich that other local denominations did not follow the example of the Presbyterians. There was a Methodist, Congregational, and Anglican church, each within two or three hundred yards from us, having between them a seating capacity of over two thousand, each happy to see a couple of dozen worshippers at any service. I have no doubt that in each of them were members advocating the acceptance of union with us on the same basis as that of the Presbyterians. Equally certainly, there were those who saw themselves wielding the sword as latter-day St. Georges against the ecumenical dragon down the road. Most dragons have a thin time when faced with the St. Georges of this world, and we were no exception. For whatever reason, the chance was missed to make of St. Mary's an ecumenical centre in a much wider sense than is possible with just two congregations and traditions.

(b) *The team*

Here five traditions were represented, but I should make it quite clear how far each felt able, or was allowed, to overcome the restrictions imposed by his own brand of churchmanship.

The Anglicans on the staff were all of the liberal brand of theology (or if they weren't when they arrived, they either broadened out or left). The attitude adopted by St Paul's declared aim of being all things to all men. Stacey himself had an enviable capacity for adapting himself to whatever brand of churchmanship or liturgical foibles he was presented with; and most of his colleagues enjoyed this capacity to varying extents. Stacey shared my conviction that most of the matters about which members of different churches become heated – forms of worship, attitudes to the clergy, denominational customs, and so on – were quite unimportant compared with the need for different people gathered together in one place to work together for the benefit of the community as a whole. One of the Anglicans on the staff described Stacey as 'liturgically illiterate', and certainly most of the principles which I outlined in my book *The Liturgical Movement and Methodism* would not have sparked off any particular train of thought in his mind. At one time this would have exasperated me, but not any more. The most important contribution made by this Movement is its insistence that whatever a congregation does in worship should be joint action with full participation of the body. Thus it militates against the 'scandal of the particular' in worship, insisting that all worshippers must accept responsibility for what occurs; and the Anglican members of the staff shared this conviction. What problems in churchmanship occurred, therefore, were provoked not by the Anglicans, but by the sense of responsibility which other members of the team felt to their own brand of churchmanship.

The two of whom this was specially true were Derek Baker and Brian Challis. As I have indicated, Baker took no step without intense forethought and discussion. He was in a different position from the rest of us, having a congregation constantly around him to whom he naturally felt responsible. He had to be on his guard to indicate to them that he was in no way being engulfed by Anglicanism, and therefore he held back from any action which was against the rules of either the Presbyterian Church or the Church of England. While this, as I have said, prevented his communicating at the staff Eucharist when this took the Anglican form, it did not prevent occasional joint communion services for the two congregations.

Challis had no congregation to keep an eye on him, but the Baptist officials amply compensated for this. He was allowed to join the staff only on condition that his membership was placed in a Baptist church. The local Baptist churches were all dominated by ultra-evangelicalism, and would have none of him. They did not, so far as I am aware, read the funeral service over him, but I have no doubt that if there had been liturgical provision for this, they would have done so. Whatever differences existed between Stacey and the devil were not immediately apparent to our local Baptists; therefore, to be associated with him was viewed as a Faustian activity. So Challis was compelled to have his membership artificially placed in a City church; and inevitably this lessened his effectiveness in the team, and nullified what could have been a massive ecumenical break-through.

Henri was in a somewhat different position. He had the support, in joining our staff, of the Apostolic Delegate in London; the Archbishop of Southwark, however, belonged to a generation to whom such action as Henri proposed taking, when his desire to join us was first mooted, was incomprehensible if not anathema. That Henri did not communicate at the staff Eucharist is not, therefore, to be wondered at; it was a matter of joy to us that he was present at all, and that in addition he took his turn in conducting and preaching at the evening service. During his time on the staff, our relationships with the local Roman Catholics, which had always been fair but never profound, became more cordial, and Stacey, Baker and I myself all shared in celebrating the Mass during the final year. It is one of the sadder ironies of the Woolwich experiment that Henri, who was unquestionably the most radical of us all in his thinking (his comments on English Roman Catholicism could not be printed, even in this book) joined us at the moment when several of us were contemplating our departure. Had he been with us from the start, some of the failures to think in depth which typified various decisions, activities, and relationships with local churches would have been avoided. He was older, and wiser, than us all; we needed him.

My position was a happier one, since I had the authority and support of the Methodist Conference behind me. In practical terms this meant that I reported regularly to the Chairman of the London South-East District, Ronald Ducker, whose goodwill and cordial support throughout the four years helped to keep the way smooth. The fact is that I was the first Free Church minister to serve on an Anglican staff, and because of this I must now describe exactly how I functioned at St. Mary's.

We had two somewhat conflicting aims in mind: not to give needless offence, and yet that I should be recognized as being as fully a minister of the Gospel as were the Anglican members of the team. Outside the Eucharist there was no problem, and I took my full share in leading the statutory services. For the first two years, I shared in the Eucharist as far as the Prayer of Thanksgiving only. I think that if I had insisted, provision would have been made for me to go further than this: neither staff, PCC nor the congregation generally would have denied me. But those were early days, and I was at that time opposed in any case to any action which might be interpreted as 'jumping the gun'. Whether as compensation for this, or because it was appreciated that Methodists lay greater emphasis on sermons than do Anglicans, I was given more than my fair share of preaching during this period.

The main pressure to extend my sphere of operation came from the Anglican congregation. They felt (as did some Methodist colleagues) that my inaction at the central part of the Eucharist was doing me some kind of despite. I was personally unaffected by this argument, but by 1966 had reached a point of no-concern about church orders. I had been a convinced ecumenist since leaving theological college, and had followed the Anglican-Methodist Conversations with considerable enthusiasm. However, as these, following the pleas and arguments presented by members of their respective commissions, became increasingly bogged down in matters of church order, status, and theological niceties, I was overtaken by the realization of how petty, trivial, meaningless and, above all, irrelevant to the historic mission of the Church in the world these arguments were. Those who presented them seemed somehow to have convinced themselves that the Church's continued existence was of divine right; that it had an independent *raison d'être* unrelated to the world from which its members came and to which they belonged: and that it was of no consequence how long they spent in putting their own houses in order. (No wonder few of my colleagues at Woolwich College for Further Education had even heard of the Conversations! Even less wonder that the few who had were disinterested. How anyone can imagine that in a troubled and divided world people will listen to the utterances of such divided people is beyond my capacity to grasp. The most we could proclaim with integrity would be 'Do as we say, not as we do'.)

So, as the Conversations became bogged down in arid legalities, and as the original spark of genuine goodwill with which the discussions had started so many years earlier seemed to be extinguished by the cold water of self-determined principles, I concluded that so far as I was concerned the existing situation with which I was immediately confronted was all that was of any real importance. In this situation, denominational differences were either not appreciated, or were ignored: at least one group of people gathered in one place were determined that the ecclesiastical strait-jacket which they had inherited should be discarded once and for all.

With this in mind, I therefore accepted the PCC's invitation to share in administering the elements, and to find a way whereby I could join in leading the whole communion service. This was achieved by a series of virtual con-celebrations at the critical points in the service.

Obviously, we could neither seek nor receive official approval for this action. Yet I believe it marks the one way forward for all those local churches who have been frustrated in their plans for unity by the failure of the Report on the Conversations to receive the approval necessary for its acceptance. If those in the higher echelons cannot reach agreement, let those at ground level go ahead and express the unity they have found. Let church orders and legal regulations be scrapped; let them be burnt in market places up and down the land. Let there be a massive series of sanctified bluff-calling expressed by men and women who, tired of obedience to an outmoded ecclesiasticism which has become a scandal in our time, wish to replace this with obedience to the needs of the age. Together, Christians may go forward to an understanding of a new type of churchmanship – better expressed, as I shall suggest in the next section, as non-churchmanship; on their own they will only fossilize in the stagnant waters of received sectarian tradition.

3. *The ordained ministry*

While we were never without team members whose sole activities related directly to the church, the majority, from 1965 on at least, earned their living in other spheres. Stacey spent a good deal of his time writing; I was editor, teacher, lecturer; there were several other teachers; one worked with a housing association, another was a local government officer, another in sociological work. The aim was to cover as many facets in local life as possible, especially where these involved direct contact with people. I suppose that ideally we should have included a doctor, works manager, shop steward, on the staff, but, as it happened, nobody with these qualifications came forward.

The issue that this naturally raised was a dual one: did those who were ordained bring anything into their secular jobs *qua* ordained men; and did the lay members of staff lack in essence anything possessed by the ordained members?

So far as the four years of the Woolwich experiment are concerned, it is impossible to give an answer which applies to the whole period; all I can do is to outline the direction in which our thinking was going, and then to add my own conclusions. Within the staff, as indicated, my own functions became increasingly those of an ordained Anglican priest, without my having been so ordained. Similarly, while we stopped short of allowing lay members to celebrate the Eucharist, Barbara Wollestan (for instance) acted as deacon, and preached, as regularly as the rest of us. We were in fact moving to a totally *functional* view of the ministry, whereby whoever was seen in a local community to possess the right gifts should be freely allowed to lead that community in worship and any other of its activities. The gifts, the need, the occasion – these, not the ceremony of ordination, produced the minister. The call, in other words, was from 'below' not from above: this was the majority, though not unanimous, view of the team.

This approach also applied to the other side of the issue: those of us working in 'secular' spheres sought to be judged only on our ability to perform the tasks we were assigned. My own view of the matter was that once I was in the lecture room my effectiveness must spring from my teaching ability. Any aura which I might possess in the eyes of some because of my ordination must be played down. (In fact, few students, and fewer staff, were conscious in general of any such aura.) Unless it happened to relate to the topic under discussion, my church background was rigorously barred from the lecture room.

28

In what ways, then, was I different from any other lecturer in the department, who had arrived there following three years in a college of education rather than a theological college? The answer lies in the realm of the empirical rather than the ontological. My training as a minister had been strongly motivated by the sense of service which the very title suggests. My work as a minister had brought me into contact with many different ages and types of people: manual workers, managing directors, professional and working class, very old and very young, and so on. I am certain that both of these factors contributed – and still do – to whatever effectiveness there was in my teaching. This is not to say that teachers do not frequently share these gifts; but it is on the cards that a young man who has gone through school, on to training college, and then into teaching will have a more limited range of 'sympathy' (in the sense of being open to other people) than will a minister of the Church. But it should be stressed that this advantage is not universal, and is in many instances only temporary.

What I know many people hoped I would say about my work was that I was 'the man of God' in the place, in a way that no layman could ever be. John Stacey expresses this 'ontological' view of the ministry when he writes:

> Perhaps the real difference (between a minister and a layman) can be expressed by saying that the minister is a sacramental person in a sense that a layman cannot be.[1]

Those who looked for this quality in my college work were disappointed. Welfare work was in the hands of an ex-Marxist Jew, a man of deep human understanding, genuine concern for the students, indifferent to the amount of time involved in this work, which was additional to his lecturing. Had I wished, I suppose I could have held a communion service on the premises occasionally as did a local R.C. priest. Apart from the fact that there were few dedicated Christians in the college, and that the system of day release gives one virtually five sets of student populations per week, my own view was that this would have been theologically unsound. I met every week about a hundred and fifty students in liberal studies classes. The themes we covered, and the type of relationships made possible in such classes, gave plenty of scope for developing the unity and the breaking down of barriers symbolized in the communion service. To have encouraged a tiny percentage of the students to meet separately at the Eucharist would have introduced a divisive element without any justifying compensation.

This view was shared by those colleagues on the St. Mary's staff exercising a similar type of ministry. Our view was that it was the existence of the team, our belonging and loyalty to it, the extent to which it was the base from which we operated, and to which we turned in order to share together the potentialities and frustrations of our work, which created any distinction between us and our colleagues at work. Ideally, it was the area where tensions could be released, and new ideas conceived. Week by week in the staff meetings a variety of mental abilities, possessed by men and women engaged in a number of different spheres which demanded a wide range of aptitudes, skills and personalities, were brought to bear for a short time (and, in exceptional circumstances, for a whole evening) on the issues faced by each member in his or her daily job.

Looking back, it now seems that we were unwittingly approaching the New Testament expression of the variety of ministries. We had those with the gift of teaching, of administration, of preaching, of compassion, and each was trying to use his gift in the area where it was most needed and could be most comprehensively expressed. There was no sense of superiority among us resulting from the work we were doing; no sense that any function was more holy than another. I have pointed out that Stacey's position as rector gave him, in some eyes, a more exalted position than some others in the team. But this was accidental to our situation, not integral to it; and it did not devolve from his performing the pastoral function within the congregation. This was the prime concern of Garrard, Baker, and Covington: had any of these been rector, he would have inherited the same *persona* in the eyes of some members of the congregation, and among some of the citizens and institutions of Woolwich.

It is the parson's *persona*, which has been handed on from generation to generation, that has proved in recent times a major obstacle to the Church's discharging its corporate function as expressing the mind of Christ among men. By '*persona*' I mean the image (literally the mask) which the parson bears, solely by virtue of his being 'a man of God'. It is this *persona*, not the man, that is uppermost when others confront him, just as when Olivier plays Othello we think of the Moor, not of the actor. (The better the actor, the more he is caught up in his *persona*: the bad actor is one who reminds the audience of himself, rather than the character he is attempting to portray.) Everyone has a *persona*, of course; but some can reach a greater degree of independence of it than others; or perhaps I should say that some can more easily doff the peripheral *persona* for one more basic, such as that of a civilized human being. Presumably, if we could remove *this*, we should merely express 'nature red in tooth and claw'.

Why then is the parson's *persona* so impeditive to the Church? It is because the concept that he is essentially different from the lay members has, whether he likes it or not, the effect of making lay members of congregations divest themselves of responsibilities which are as much theirs as his. So long as – in Anthony Hanson's words,[2] 'the ministry is the pioneer for Christian living for the Church'; so long as it is accepted, in John Stacey's words, that 'the ministry is used by God *because he is a minister*, and in some cases and instances, for that reason alone' – so long will the majority of laymen disclaim any liability for the pastoral, administrative, sacramental and, in some denominations, preaching activities of the Church.

In other words, I am arguing that we have passed the age when these activities can be accepted as one man's sphere of operations. There was a time when this was inevitable, since the parson was the only literate member of the community. I suspect that this fact gave strong backing to the ontological view of the ministry, that the parson is essentially different from laymen. The combination of an empirical fact with a metaphysical absolute put the parson in an impregnable position; but today, with the parson not necessarily the most intellectual, nor the natural leader, of a congregation, the absolute seems to be continually presented in a vacuum. It must disappear from our thinking, and with it must go the *persona* which is, sadly, used by some parsons to give themselves a status in the community which they could not naturally bear.

John Stacey argues[3] that this functional view of the ministry leaves as a debatable point what functions shall be included, for anyone to qualify. I prefer to look at the matter in reverse: any man (or woman) who sees his sphere of work as the area of dedicated service to which he is committed, and is prepared to share some common discipline with others in his vicinity who share this sense of service, is a minister of that group in the sense that this is the base from which he serves, or ministers to, people day by day. I recognize that, for the time being, the need exists for some men's sphere of service to be within a congregation. But I foresee that as these gradually dwindle away, they will be replaced by small groups, with one of their members as co-ordinator or convenor. What is likely to be the basis of their common convictions I shall discuss later. Already one hears of 'non-church' groups of this kind meeting in Britain, America, and other countries. We made a step in this direction at Woolwich.

It is relevant at this stage to outline my own view of the future development of the ministry. I see the profession becoming increasingly involved in a deadly paradox: that of being functionaries without any obvious function. So long as there was no widespread objection to the ontological view of the ministers as the representatives of God among men, the question of their actual functions was, while not unimportant, secondary to their basic *raison d'être*. With the evaporation of the priestly image, this second factor comes inevitably into prominence. What will ministers do in an age when the organization to which they are attached – the Church – is steadily dwindling? Is there any justification for their continued existence, and, if so, how will they be supported? There is a certain natural adjustment occurring, of course: with the decline in church attendance, there has been a commensurate decline in the number of candidates for the ministry. But to accept this as having come to terms with the problem is avoiding the main issue: is there no quality in life that the ministry has hitherto represented which is not still needed in the human situation?

There are certain qualities traditionally associated with the clergy which we shall all be better off without. I include here the type of authoritarianism expressed by the hierarchy of the Roman Catholic Church, which on the birth control issue is encouraging the human species to rush down the slope that leads to world over-population, with its attendant starvation, violence, and paucity of life. There is the type of authority expressed by the Church of England when it is in an establishment-minded mood. These occasions are becoming mercifully rarer as the Church's general authority diminishes, but the sense of being 'born to rule' possessed by some of the dignitaries and other clergy was the aspect of Anglicanism which I found most excruciating during my association with that Church. There is the authoritarianism of the Billy Grahams of this world, waving their Bibles aloft like special constables' handbooks. It will be a happy day when we know that we shall hear no more utterances beginning 'The Bible says . . .' – meaning 'This is what I think of current trends in the moral situation'.

The ministry, however, has always had in its midst men who have heartily rejected all these expressions of authority. It has included not only the inadequate but also men of great ability and insight; not only the humble and unimportant (as men assess

32

others) but also natural leaders and pioneers; those who act, besides those who only react. What are such men to do, and how are such gifts to find expression in the future? Monica Furlong has suggested[4] that we need men who are free 'to be rather than to do' – free for others rather than having compulsory duties to fulfil each day, men who are 'available' ('disponible' as the Taizé Community affirm). How will such men be found if in the future there is no Church to sustain them?

The answer is that men possessing gifts of sympathy and understanding, rare and precious commodities in any community, will continue to bear the stamp whatever work they are doing. As a matter of fact, apart from those in rural Anglican parishes (and not always there) most ministers could hardly claim to be 'available' for most of their time. I doubt if anyone's diary is fuller than that of the average minister, so that the actual hours that he can spend with people who require someone to listen to them are not likely to be more than, say, a shop steward or personnel officer in industry, a teacher or lecturer, or a social worker. The hours which a minister is compelled to spend in administration, and the routine activities of church life, are not diminishing but growing in number as the attendances shrink and it becomes increasingly difficult to maintain buildings. (It is this fact more than any other which brings about such speedy disillusionment in the minds of many young ministers after leaving theological college.)

A significant question to ask is whether, with the decline in the number of candidates for the ministry, the valuable qualities which I mentioned earlier are beginning to disappear from modern society. The answer is that of course they are not. It is only that more and more of the young men possessing these qualities, who in earlier generations would have seen the ministry as their natural area of service, are turning now to other spheres where, as some have expressed it to me, there is more opportunity to express their gifts. Even in 1965, when my thinking had not reached its present position, I counselled, in a careers book on the ministry, *Rev*[5], that, because I foresaw the 'worker-priest' style of ministry becoming more universal, it was strongly advisable if not essential for any potential candidate for the ministry first to gain experience and qualification in some other profession or skill. He would then never be in the position of some in the ministry today who feel that full-time activity in the Church is no longer justified, but have no qualification for anything else.

What will disappear, then, is not the human gifts which many ministers have possessed in every generation, but the concentration of these gifts on those who happen to spend a certain proportion of their time in the activities revolving around church buildings. I suspect that this would already have happened more widely than it has, were it not for the practice of ordination, with the mystical image attached to it. This concept exemplifies the stages of development of all metaphysical concepts. An existing situation evokes certain necessary practices, rules, or ideas. These then become formalized, and the society which so proceeds looks for some means of perpetuating them. This is achieved by overlaying the particular practice or rule with a mythological image, independent of time and place. Customs change with the passing years; the rules or practices relate less and less to developing societies; but because the various myths have persisted, the practices associated with them continue to seem necessary and justified. This is as true of 'God', moral absolutes, even aesthetic principles, as it is of ordination.

Without the metaphysical concept of ordination (devolving from the metaphysical concept of God) the ministry would not survive. The only quality which gives any meaning to the minister's ecclesiastical functions is the myth. Remove this, and you are left with an occasionally helpful but predominantly pointless round of duties, from which anyone with any real sense of service to the community would thankfully escape into another sphere. In other words, there would, without ordination, be a greater spur for men to become more dedicated in those spheres where the need is greatest – in housing, urban development with its accompanying violence and loneliness, in racialist areas, and so on. The furthering of human needs in these contexts would increasingly be recognized as the area for the modern ministry of sympathy and compassion; any encouragement to neglect these in favour of an ecclesiastical machine which has long since ceased to serve the community in which it is placed must therefore be viewed as a tantalizing diversion. It is one of the pieces of evidence which leads me, reluctantly but inexorably, to the conclusion that 'religion' (in the traditional sense of that word) is more than just irrelevant in modern society: it is a barrier to human progress.

This raises the question of theological colleges or seminaries. Already the advisability of these as separate entities has been under review by the World Council of Churches,[6] and in America there have been moves to merge theology, in universities, with related disciplines. At Bristol University, the theological department is moving towards the unity of the 'pastoral' professions, having joint degrees in theology and philosophy, and joint seminars with the departments of Social Administration, Architecture, and Mental Health. This seems to be the right context for theological study and the distinctive disciplines which it embodies. The intellectual link between systematic theology and philosophy, and the practical link between pastoral theology and sociology, raise the inevitable question of why this kind of step has not been taken earlier and more universally. It could provide precisely the kind of training required by any young man enthusiastic enough to discover a salve to the world's diseases. As Gibson Winter has written:

> At present, men prepare for the role of religious specialist as though they were to be *ministers* of the Church. At every step of their preparation for the initial struggle to share in a private language up to the donning of special clothes or a peculiar liquidity of intonation, the religious specialist is separated from the historical struggle of the world. The prophetic fellowship has no place for such spokesmen for private, religious culture; it desperately needs men who are engaged in the historical struggle rather than fleeing from it; it calls for men and women who are open to history . . . The Church in a secular world needs specialists who are willing to be auxiliary aids to the laity rather than attempting to enlist the laity as auxiliaries to their organizational enterprise.[7]

There are differences of emphasis between this approach and mine, since Winter views the Church as the ongoing 'prophetic fellowship': but within the context of the new groupings which I shall later describe, this appears to be a fine statement of the right motivation for anyone today who feels that his particular personality and gifts can most extensively be used in some kind of community service.

That some of the qualities historically associated with the clergy are still required in human life is evident from these words by Monica Furlong, the Anglican journalist, writing in *New Christian*:

> I am clear what I want from the clergy. I want them to be people who can by their own happiness and contentment challenge my ideas about status, about success, about money, and so teach me how to live more independently of such

drugs. I want them to be people who can dare, as I do not
dare, and as few of my contemporaries dare, to refuse to
work flat out (since work is an even more subtle drug than
status), to refuse to compete with me in strenuousness. I
want them to be people who are secure enough in the value
of what they are doing to have time to read, to sit and
think, and who can face the emptiness and possible depres-
sion which often attack people when they do not keep the
surface of their mind occupied . . . I want them to be people
who can sit still without feeling guilty, and from whom I can
learn some kind of tranquillity in a society which has almost
lost the art.[8]

My comments on Miss Furlong's splendid words are threefold.
   Firstly, however valuable the qualities she describes may be,
the ordained ministry has not, and never has had, a monopoly
on them. There are plenty of non-religious people who have
grasped and expressed the truth of which she writes. They are to
be found in any profession and in people of varying opinions and
convictions – including those for whom the term 'God' is
meaningless.
   Secondly, in choosing the ordained ministry as exemplifying
her ideal (even if not universally) she displays considerable ignorance of the facts. By what right can ministers decry the lure
of money, and belittle the need for material security, when they
themselves have, short of the rarest circumstances, security for
life and (when the hidden benefits such as a free house are taken
into account) an income well above the average in the community?[9] What can the majority of ministers say against working
flat out when they themselves are putting in more hours daily
than most members of their congregations, or of the community
at large? What have they to offer against status-seeking when, in
the largest Church in England at least, 'preferment' is accepted
as part of the system?
   Thirdly, and fundamentally, it seems misconceived to want to
encourage the setting apart of a few in order to 'sit and think' if
the motive is that they shall convey the value of this to others with
routine functions to perform. Most people with a modicum of
common sense will agree that this is valuable; the problem is not
one of convincing them about this, but giving them the opportunity. Unless the 'scandal of the particular' is again accepted, to
single out a few for special favour can add nothing constructive
to the contemporary situation.

Shall we say, then, that the motive for setting people apart in this way is that they may reflect on contemporary problems from a distance, and offer their objective comments on how to solve them? Most disciplines have their specialists who are given university or college posts with this function primarily in mind, though it is questionable how far their thinking gets through to those actually working at the coal face. Writing of education, for instance, the Professor of Education at York says:

> It may have been hoped at one time that educational enlightenment could be carried into schools by probationary teachers fresh from college – as if these could teach the old dogs in the staff room to perform new tricks; what normally happens is that the dogs teach the youngsters some useful old ones.
>
> But reform, however, can result if we organize a two-way traffic across the gap between schools on the one side and colleges, institutes and departments on the other. At present it is far too rare for a class teacher to play an active and recognized part in training recruits for the profession; for a tutor or lecturer to be involved with the regular task of classroom teaching; for teachers to go on the kind of courses which will send them back richer in mind and purse to the classroom.[10]

The same kind of gulf exists in the world of theology – perhaps more so. What would be the reaction of the average member of a congregation if he could hear some of the lectures delivered in theological colleges? How many ministers dare state from the pulpit biblical or doctrinal views being propagated by those 'set apart'? And Miss Furlong wants all her ministers in this category!

It would appear more consistent with what human beings require to accept what may be loosely described as incarnational theology. In other words, you recognize that for the vast majority of people this tranquillity, if it is to be found at all, must be experienced as an inner reality amid the daily round of living. True peace of mind does not evolve by escaping from this; it is an inward assurance which can sustain and strengthen amid all the tensions of life, which most men must expect to experience. It is found, not by escaping from life, but in and through it. Isaiah expressed this concept when he said,[11] 'Pass through water, and I will be with thee, so that the flood shall not drown thee; walk amid the flames, and thou shalt not be burnt, the fire shall have no power to catch thee.'

It was also expressed by the atheist Camus in this way: 'In the middle of winter, I at last found that there was in me an invincible summer.'[12] To experience this is the birthright of all, not a select few.

While I have clearly taken the argument in these last few pages beyond the particular insights of the Woolwich experiment, I found the trend which it expressed to be away from the circuit, or parochial, ministry. Most of those who were formerly on the staff are no longer engaged in this. If it be argued – as it is, particularly by older members of the profession – that we were discounting those (and they are many) still engaged in church-centred work, the answer is that our attitude towards these ranged from admiration to pity: admiration for those who, despite all the frustrations of the job, were still exhibiting the rare qualities of dedication and compassion; and pity for those who no longer believed in their job, but – either because of age or for lack of qualifications – had nowhere else to go, and were simply looking forward to retirement.

Our attitude to young would-be ministers was, as indicated, that they should first work for qualifications outside theology. I would now add to this that if they then proceed to a study of theology (hopefully in the wider context outlined earlier) they should at the end remain as laymen. By so doing they would be helping to destroy the distinction between clergy and laity brought about by the ontological view of ordination; and they would be making themselves available for full-time service in a sphere in which the human contacts would not be limited to those with the habit of attending church. Since I now view ordination as simply the seal or approval of fitness to serve, made on behalf of those to be served, and since I foresee no future for the organization in which this approval is given, it would be somewhat inconsistent on my part if I recommended otherwise.

4. *The Group*

This last insight of the Woolwich experiment need only be briefly mentioned here, since it is the theme of the next section. It will already have become apparent to most readers that the Woolwich team, by 1967, were well on their way to being an *ecclesiola in ecclesia*. As time went by we – or most of us – increasingly felt that our prime loyalty was towards the team which, while not completely detached from the church as locally represented, was moving ever further out on a limb in relation to it.

On reflection, it now seems to me that those in the future who despair of the Church to the point of wishing no longer to be identified with it, but who are not prepared to take the theological and practical steps to be discussed in the next two sections, may find that some form of common commitment to a group of others who, in this way (though not necessarily in every way) share their convictions, may be the answer to their dilemma. One essential difference between such groups and normal church congregations is that the members choose those to whom they wish to be committed; another is that there is no tradition dominating their activities, so that they are free to act entirely according to the wishes of the members, and the exigencies of the local situation. This adaptability enables a group to exercise a pragmatic approach in its thinking and actions; and the ability to dispense with the secondary, the unimportant, and the pointless can give their decisions a meaning, both to themselves and to the community generally, which makes for an existentialist situation.

A number of such groups, Christian in conviction but unattached to any church, are springing up in America. One example is the Sycamore Community in Pennsylvania. One of their early statements outlined their aims:

> The Sycamore Community is a handful of Christian laymen. It has no building – but access to all those which a modern town provides; it has no money, except our salaries; it has no financial resources, but access to all the power of modern society; it has no program, except to serve human need in the context of the Christian faith. We regard ourselves as an attempt – one experiment to find a new pattern of Christian life together appropriate to our science-technology-determined culture....
>
> What are our collective missions? Because we have no city slum to clear up, we naturally felt disadvantaged! ! ... Instead, our servanthood has taken the form of being the clearing house and agent for the small groups and experimental ministries of all kinds. ... We frankly find such a mission less emotionally fulfilling than the personal experiences of counselling, prison visitation, etc., in which we are involved as individuals – but *perhaps* it is *our* mission at this time.[13]

Since they were antipathetic to church buildings, this group took a half-page advertisement in the local paper protesting against the building of a 1.3 million dollar church. They also advertised for any clergy who felt that they could no longer fulfil a ministry in the Church to come out. One hundred of the clergy replied, sixty-five of whom (according to Professor Roy of the local university, one of the pioneers of the group) eventually left their churches to conduct a ministry in 'secular' occupations. Some of these were found their jobs by the community.

There are other similar expressions of these 'extra-ecclesiastical churches' or 'Christian outsiders' or 'New-formers', as they are termed in America: there is the San Francisco venture which meets weekly for worship and study, and has worked in the neighbourhood to create a study centre for children, voter registration, and to help children to work with art and creative expression. Another example is in Rochester N.Y. under the name 'Ekklesia'. Professor Roy admits, in a recent letter to me, that there has been, generally speaking, 'a slight reversion to compromise solutions with the ongoing structures. There are probably half-a-dozen identifiable Christian Congregations not attached to any denomination but very explicitly part of the *Church*. We would welcome Charles Davis into membership.'

It is highly significant that groups like these, together with the forms of religio-political commitment which will be considered in section three, are to be found in a country which, although church attendance shows a very slight decline year by year (49 per cent of the population in 1955, 44 per cent in 1966), makes English churches look empty in comparison. It indicates that the motivation for radical or revolutionary change cannot be written off, as some are ready to do, as just a case of deserting when under fire. Here is one comment based on this opinion:

> To leave (the Church) is to behave like the crew lost in fog, who abandon ship and leave the blind, who do not see the fog, and the crippled, who cannot help themselves, to drift on with the ship.[14]

Apart from the fact that the estimation of church members revealed in this outburst could hardly be lower, the choice of metaphor seems unfortunate, in view of the fact that passengers on board a ship must, willy-nilly, for the duration of a voyage treat the ship as their world.

To ask the question, therefore, whether the St. Mary's team would have moved so far from the congregation and begun to form itself into an extra-ecclesiastical group if the Church itself had been thriving, socially active, theologically alert is to put a non-question. If this had been the case, then many of the Church members would themselves have constituted the team. Our reasons for taking the direction we did (insofar as they were consciously formulated in our minds at all) were that the Church was not doing the job for which it was created; that its very ecclesiasticism prevented its achieving this, diverting members into socially non-valuable activity; and that we had consequently to act according to the need as we identified it. This is certainly the motivation of the radicals and revolutionaries on the American scene: their context, or base, is not the Church, which remains largely indifferent to and independent of the social and political upheavals presently convulsing the whole country, but society in general and in particular that radical element in it which is aiming to be the catalyst of a new society.

Whether we at St. Mary's were even beginning to act in this capacity in Woolwich is impossible to say. Perhaps it was the wrong area in which to operate, since in many ways our most effective contribution to the area was in the new town of Thamesmead, in the planning for which Barbara Wollestan, Derek Baker and Nick Stacey were at different times active. But we could hardly all collect our gear and hive ourselves off to a new town! We had to operate where we found ourselves. Perhaps we should eventually have become more politically committed than we were; it is on the cards, for instance, that Jeremy Hurst would, sooner or later, have been nominated for the local Council. The fact remains that four years is too short a time to be able to assess influence empirically. Any point of view about this would be purely subjective, and likely to be based more on wishful thinking than on reality.

As a postscript to this section, it can be added that so far as the Church is concerned, the Woolwich experiment has died, and there has been no attempt to resurrect it, either in a different form elsewhere, or with different personnel on the same base. Following Stacey's departure, those concerned with appointments ensured that St. Mary's would return to more tranquil waters, and reports confirm my personal impression that every attempt has been made to return to the *status quo ante*. The two legacies of the team which alone survive are the restructured buildings and the presence of the Presbyterians. This is not surprising since, as I conceded in my fourth comment on the Woolwich contribution, the most important developments in the team required an independent framework, an expression wider than the Church. I think I was the first to appreciate this; but already most of the team members are looking for this wider expression. To the extent that being a member of the team helped these ideas to crystallize (since no ideas in this direction, however 'way out' or far-fetched, were treated in the team with less than serious attention) we are all indebted to it; and to the extent that its insights are maintained by its members, or taken up by others in different fields, it may yet be prophetic for the community as a whole.

THE NON-CHURCH

THE phrase 'the non-church' will conjure up a variety of images according to the mind of the reader. Those who have heard of the movement in Japan called *Mukyokai*[1] will have some idea of a back-to-the-Bible movement; others will view it as an anti-church movement, and therefore perhaps more appropriate on the lips of humanists or atheists than on those of people in any way connected with the Church; others will simply look upon it as a totally meaningless phrase. It seems appropriate, therefore, to outline events which started in 1966, to which the concept of non-church was central.

On 2 June 1966 an article of mine appeared in the radical religious journal *New Christian* entitled 'The Coming Non-Church'. This article was the successor to an earlier one in *Prism* (*New Christian*'s sire) facing the question of whether Methodism could survive until full organic union with the Anglican Church, assuming that this would take fifteen to twenty years. The conclusion reached in that earlier article was that it could not survive, and as a result I received numerous letters criticizing the article for its negative and destructive tone. If Methodism – and, by implication, the other denominations – could not survive, it was asked, what was envisaged replacing them? The article on 'Non-Church' was an attempt to face this question.

It seemed essential to be clear from the start about the motivation of those still convinced that Christianity had a part to play in human life. The basic aim, it seemed, was to escape from a church-centred motivation. This was primarily because for an increasing number of people, especially among the younger section of society, the church organization no longer represented in their eyes that which had inspired its origins. I wrote:

> The image of the church in most people's minds is of a well-meaning but ineffectual organization; it may not do much harm, but it is an anachronism in contemporary society.

So the article went on to outline in general terms the direction in which I felt those should be looking who agreed with this assessment:

What Christians need today most of all is the determination that the love which was seen in Jesus Christ shall become real among men, *whether they recognize the source of it or not.* Our task is not to baptize but to make the good news known; not to bring people to church but to take its essential power to them; not to induce guilt complexes but to help people find the essential depths in themselves: not to talk theology – perhaps not even to talk at all – but to express in ourselves, and by the decisions we arrive at as the result of our thinking together, what good neighbourliness means in social, industrial, commercial, educational, and personal life.

In short, our task is to humanize the monsters of our age, so that the full personality of man can begin to flower. In Jesus Christ this is possible, for in him the new humanity has been seen and expressed; but the tragedy and irony is that the Church which contains this mystery and therefore ought to be the universal guide into the truth has, through its established position, its top-heavy organization and its crass pettifogging rules, become a monster in its own right.

Consideration was then given to three of the main visible causes of the Church's malaise (ideas which arose, as section one of this book has indicated, largely from my experiences in Woolwich): its divisions, its multiplicity of buildings, and its professional clergy. The article concluded:

It may well be that we are in for a period when there will be no clearly-defined pattern of the Church at all. In some places it may be that ad hoc groups, chosen from local personnel (in a factory or a school, for instance) will meet occasionally to discuss how love can be expressed in their situation (though they will probably not speak of it in those terms). *And for these people this will be the Church.* Elsewhere groups may gather for informal times of discussion or worship in the homes of those who give the lead. For them this will be the Church. Others again may wish to meet occasionally for a celebration of the Eucharist. . . . But these may well be a minority of the whole.

I foresee the breaking down of central structures, and the springing into life of local expressions of the Christian community, with different communities varying considerably from one another. The danger of wrong beliefs and practices creeping into such a situation are offset by the inevitable freedom from the dead hand of conformity which must accrue. It may be that with such a pattern the Church will once again begin to stand for something which is real in men's lives, instead of standing as the guardian of a tradition which is generally rejected because its essential worth is hidden behind ecclesiastical jargon, imposing edifices and clerical collars.

The Church is dead. Long live the non-church!

The article had hinted earlier that the problem facing the Church was theological rather than liturgical or ecclesiastical; this was an issue which had to be faced eventually, but as it did not emerge straightaway as the main talking-point, it is better that we leave that particular discussion until section three, and recount here points of view and events as they were made or happened.

The central issue which sparked off a good deal of interest was that of who was, or would be, in the non-church. My purpose in coining this particular title was to stress the fact of the artificiality of the so-called distinction between many church-goers and 'outsiders', Christians and non-Christians. The differences between these two, when the great human issues of our time were under discussion, looked threadbare. On problems such as housing, race, world poverty, war, urban tensions, there was often little to choose, both in theory and practice, between these two groupings. Of course, one group went to church and the other didn't; one professed a belief in God and the divinity of Jesus Christ, while the other generally did not. But the first distinction affected only a couple of hours a week; and the second, so far as potential action was concerned, affected motive rather than practice: was it not possible, then, that the Church must not so much 'go out' as recognize itself as being 'out' already? Was it not even possible that some church-goers had more in common with some so-called humanists or agnostics than they had with some fellow church-goers? If so, was it not worth attempting to do something positive towards bringing the two together?

This, at any rate, was what the title implied: attempting to achieve the fruits of churchmanship without presenting the theological and ecclesiastical foundation as compulsory prerequisites of these. It was an extension of the St. Mary's team experiment, independent of the main body of the Church, but broader in scope philosophically.

One letter to *New Christian* typified comments which were to be later frequently received:

Having just read the article 'The Coming Non-Church', the possible truth that I must be one of its 'members' has occurred to me.

Although I have some good friends who are priests . . . I do not go to Church and would not normally dream of doing so. . . . I have no time for any theology or doctrine specific to any denomination. I believe that God is active, and see in Jesus Christ a person saturated with the goodness of God, and displaying His Love and Truth.

If there are going to be many Christians in a couple of decades time, I believe that they will be my sort. I am sure that most of my generation who think about these things at all, inwardly know that the Church system is either dying or dead, and we look forward to its burial, and to the coming Non-Church.

On 14 July Alison Adcock wrote her article 'Non-church is Nonsense' from which I have already quoted her defence of church buildings as places in which to unwind. Earlier in the article, she pointed out that the Quakers came nearest of all groups known to her to the non-church ideal; but that these were notoriously small in numbers. She suggested that this was in fact the nub of the matter:

The godless teenagers and the man in the street show no more signs of wanting to sit around in groups evolving ways of showing love than of wanting to attend old-fashioned Eucharists. . . . Is it perhaps the unpalatable truth that modern man doesn't want anything to do with any sort of religion, church or non-church, and if we find a form of togetherness with popular appeal it won't be religious in anybody's sense of the term?

This was a question to which those who shared my concern felt compelled to address themselves. Whether the word 'religious' would be used to define emerging groups was at that time secondary to the quest for a formula whereby they could be encouraged, or induced, to emerge in the first place. If Alison Adcock was right we should be wasting our time anyway; but it was worth a try.

I was fortunate later that year to be asked by *The Times* to provide an article on the theme of non-church, and this appeared on 11 November. After mentioning the frustration felt by many church members when facing the need for reform, I continued:

Outside the Church there must be many who, because they recognize in Jesus Christ a positive affirmation, would like to call themselves Christians but are deterred by the existing Church from making such a claim. It is clear that these two groups – those just inside and those just outside the Church – have much in common; they are, or could be, a body of 'christians'.

I then outlined what at that time I considered would be the five distinguishing signs of this new group:

1. It would be centred on the person of Jesus Christ, not in the sense of 'I believe', because credal statements, however high-sounding, have no importance in themselves, but only when translated into behaviour and character. As Nietzsche said: 'I will not believe in a Redeemer until I see a company of people who are redeemed.' We need people who affirm that in Jesus Christ life is seen at its best, so that by committing oneself to such a life one is seeking to enter into the fullness of existence – what Jesus himself called 'abundant life'.

2. It would allow for the meeting together, as often as may be desired, of people in natural groupings: at work, at college, in homes, or in a hired room if necessary. There would be no buildings specially set apart for these meetings which would be cellular, being constituted of people who are part of that place at that time (that is, they live, work, or study in that area).

3. The aim and purpose of the meeting would be to consider the problems – personal, social, economic, etc., – facing the members; it would allow for an unhurried study of the issues concerned, and a thorough airing of views. Each would help the others according to his understanding and experience. The Christian tradition might be considered by reference to the Bible or to history, and the presence of at least one person theologically trained would therefore be valuable. Because there might well be times of silence as well as of speech, it could be that eventually a type of worship would emerge – but only if it was a natural expression of what the group needed.

4. There would be no ordained or separated leader. Instead, any natural leader would emerge by right, and the group would probably get off the ground only because of such a person. In other words, the non-church would openly

depend on personality instead of office or function, and this would be the key to its effectiveness.

5. There would be no permanent organization. Cells must be a natural occurrence, happening only where people are, and when people wish. If key people moved away, one cell might cease to function while another came into existence.

I concluded:

It would thus give basic Christianity – the expression of love (agape) in every sphere of life – a chance to emerge, and might be a means of reversing the trend towards a hurried, selfish, impersonal existence in society generally today. It could see the emergence of a type of worship more relevant to the world we inhabit, and more related to the real needs of participants. It would exist alongside the present ecclesiastical machine, but would not be dependent upon its survival.

For the next two or three weeks there was considerable correspondence in *The Times* on this theme, with viewpoints both for and against the proposals. On 26 November, an unsigned article was published entitled 'Reasons for non-success of the non-church'. Describing me as 'a sort of Arian Humanist' the author argued that my article misrepresented the essence of Christianity. He wrote:

To the Christian *agape* is not just human love – humanism and Christianity are not all the same thing. The New Testament meaning of the word is the love of God for men and from this comes its secondary meaning, men's love for each other – and for God. . . .

What Jesus called 'abundant life' is the gift of the spirit, and he describes it in John 14 where he talks of his imminent death and resurrection as the way he is to pour out his spirit on his disciples. . . .

Part of the early Christian meetings was a 'love supper' which followed the Eucharist. The love and fellowship they expressed in this less formal meal was a sign of the 'abundant life' they had received in the Eucharist. . . .

Christianity . . . is a living community founded on the living Christ, which is fed and made visible in the celebration of the Eucharist and its new divine life is seen in the lives of its members.

This, of course, is a statement in traditional terms of Christian

48

theology relating to the matters I had raised. But it misses the point I was making: if 'abundant life' is to be as circumscribed as this correspondent suggests, what is to be the reaction to the apparent contemporary lack of desire for it, as evinced by the declining numbers at the Eucharist? Is it really in harmony with Jesus's teaching to confine this quality to members of an ecclesiastical structure? What about the many who never go near a church but yet display what this correspondent would presumably call the 'gifts of the spirit'? Can we continue to use the 'spiritual capital' argument in an age which even the most optimistic churchman must recognize as 'post-Christian'? These are questions which must be faced at greater length in the next section: meanwhile I may briefly summarize the same writer's comments on my five 'pointers'.

On the first, the writer commented that non-church groups would be indistinguishable from a 'James Dean fan club'. With reference to the second, he defended the erection of costly church buildings with a reminder about Solomon's temple. He added: 'If today . . . cathedrals are half empty, at least they serve as a rebuke to our present day loss of faith'. (As Eric Morecambe would say, there's no answer to that.) On the third he argued in favour of a God-centred, rather than what he foresaw as a man-centred, community in the non-church. He described my fourth suggestion as having a 'familiarly fascist ring', and suggested that the leaders of the non-church would be 'first class members' like the church's priests. Finally, he criticized the cells I described as being 'man-made, not called by God.'

All these criticisms could have been – and were – foreseen, and begged a large number of questions, not least that of who is to decide what is called 'of God' and what exactly has been said when that phrase is introduced. For my part, I was heartened by the number of personal letters I received, following *The Times* article and a letter on the same theme which I wrote to *The Observer*. Over three hundred of these letters eventually arrived, and I shall quote from a handful of them in order to indicate the kind of need which was felt, and which the writers hoped would be met in the non-church. I shall comment occasionally on their views, but some points raised refer to issues which will be considered later.

This one is from an American ex-theological student:

I see the church structures, i.e. denominations, as totally irrelevant, not to be renewed, united, or whatever, but to be ignored and/or circumvented. I reject the present Church on both structural and theological grounds. But I don't reject structure and theology. I think we need to understand the Christian faith as *political theology*[2] and the structures as ensuring that this non-metaphysical theology hits home in the life of man. . . . I think of the life of the Christian today as a process of dialogue and action: dialogue instead of celebration, and action which is geared to change things in the acedic city hall to revolution in Brazil.

(I had never met the word 'acedic', and discovered that it means apathetic, or sluggish.) He concluded:

I've reread your article and think you've got something that could constitute a radical breakthrough which we ought to take as far as we can.

This letter was sent by its author to *The Observer*, but was not published:

The complete failure of theologians to help young people cope with all the added tensions arising in society today is highlighted by increased drug-taking. For this is a sickness of the spirit, in dealing with which they set themselves up as experts. Where are the modern prophets? Those who are able to *anticipate* the work of the psychiatrist, and tackle root causes rather than the sickness itself. Certainly not in the Church. Are theologians too inturned upon their own perplexities and difficulties that they have no time for the world around? No wonder there is an arising interest in a 'non-Church' – by which that which is without an institution can be considered as well as that which is within. The task of spiritual guidance is passing away from the Church into the world of men – who are far more important than any way by which a man-made institution can be preserved. For that seems to be the preoccupation of contemporary theologians.

In a private letter to me, the author of the above added:

All the 'shocking' of people going on in society today is part of the ferment taking place, as men are being compelled to take up a completely new attitude of man and at last begin to look at creation as it really is. All their inhibitions have been protective factors, so that they have to lose a certain sense of protection in the first place – just as Jesus felt abandoned and lost on the cross. This is where the agony might come in. But as more and more people begin to grasp the implications, this feeling of loneliness is reduced.

That this feeling of loneliness existed was evinced by many other letters from people who felt unable any longer to identify themselves with the Church, yet felt equally ill at ease in association with such groups as secularist or humanist organizations. They were not desirous of 'changing sides': their aim was to meet and share insights, questions, concepts, with people whose past associations would not inhibit discussion, and who would not be simply looking for a new label to pin on either themselves or others. This point of view is splendidly expressed in this letter from a man who seems to me to be a latter-day prophet:

> The world – history – now awaits a new development as different as Christianity was from Judaism, and just as much a continuation. Efforts to join up churches and so forth are wrong: wasted mind, wasted effort. People should meet to lash one another's intuitions in a genuine effort to divine out of the air of the time the new Thing, the new 'twist', equal to the Christian 'twist'. It may be the Kingdom: the world awaits *world men:* as passionately *that* as nation-men have been passionate about their nation-things. The world is one world now. There is a need for men and women to get together who have both rejected all the past but are part of all the past. Forget dead men now: forget Marx, forget the Rationalists-Humanists etc etc; let them moulder in their graves as we, the living-now, have as much time to think everything anew as any men have ever had at any time in past history. We have a more complex problem than ever any other men living had at any other time in history. This is a time for originality from YOU. Damn your blasted dead.

A letter which still retains the name 'Christian', but expresses ideas on roughly similar lines, is this from a Roman Catholic priest (who has since faced stern criticism from his community):

> I feel that there must come a positive growth towards a non-credal uninstitutionalized Christian community. At present there is little tie-up between the 'conditioned' structures (and the reasoning behind them) of our churches and that of the Gospel of Jesus – based unashamedly on fraternal principles. What you say about small groupings of Christians who gather together, and who determine their own mission frontiers, would seem to be the way that the churches should go.

This one also came from a writer with a theological background:

> Whilst studying for ordination to the Congregational ministry, I came increasingly to believe that the 'Church' is indeed fettering the work to which we are called. For this reason I resigned my position to take up a teaching course. I now feel firmly committed to the necessity for us who feel like this to act – by an immediate withdrawal of our support from active church life! There are many pockets of like-minded Christians who feel themselves to be gross heretics and yet will not voice their objections or alternatives. These must be made to see that their movement is but a segment of what is surely a fast-growing and international feeling among Christians.

Both these letters hint at the realization that a new point of departure has been reached by the race as a whole, and that within this situation the Christian Church has no contribution to make. This point is pursued in the final letter that I will quote, though here the basic theoretical approach is somewhat different:

> Toynbee, in his 'Study of History', describes those junctures in which societies come to be ready for a new departure in spiritual matters, and it has seemed to me that we live at just such a time. The scales of ancient conformities are cast from our eyes. We could be – as few generations have ever seemed to be – unusually free to find new ways of looking at old truths.
> My personal anxiety is that the cells you propose could too easily fall into a new pretended knowledge of the nature and purpose of God, and give rise to another false theology. I feel that a creature (i.e. a created being) in a closed creation (i.e. one confined by life and death, and isolated in endless time and space) cannot expect to find within his experience the means to explain himself, and far less his creator, and whatever purposes he may have. If the 'non-church' could have an 'atheology' and live in the simple faith 'He is; I am His' I need it very much indeed.

These letters all in various ways expressed the conviction that for too long Christians and humanists had been segregated because of (as the writers believed) an over-emphasis on theory, which clearly divided the two, and a relative disregard for practice, on which the two were frequently united. The majority of the letters received were either from church members who were disillusioned far beyond the stage of, for instance, the Renewal Group (with their eager attempts to sharpen up the Church's wits, and to give the whole structure a fresh coat of paint, prior to taking over the running of it); or they were from those so thoroughly disenchanted with the Church that they had left it altogether. Few letters were received from actual humanists, undoubtedly because the titles of my articles would simply not have attracted their attention. After all, my own background was in the Church, and this was the area of my particular disenchantment. However, some humanists did write, including one who said:

> I recognise that you are on to a really good idea, and I guess that a number of the humanist groups that seem to be arising nowadays will be good territory for you.

That this could well be true is given substance in an article in *Prism* by the secretary of the Ethical Union and director of the British Humanist Association, H. A. Blackhan:

> To be a Christian, says Montaigne, is to be more than ordinarily just, charitable, kind. In practice this may be so, and one might say that in practice to be a humanist is to be more than ordinarily honest-minded, public-spirited, tolerant. It does not sound as nice, but the comparison in practice would probably yield fairly even marks, and anyhow, the words would have to be spelled out before comment is profitable. But faith without works is not Christianity, and unbelief without any effort to help shoulder the consequences for mankind is not humanism. If one wakes up from a sense of unlimited dependence to a supposed independence, instead of unlimited interdependence, it is simply to change illusions, for the worse.[3]

There will always be those within the Church who consider that any *modus vivendi* that is established between Christians and humanists will be through the sacrifice of the former rather than the latter. Leaving this point aside for the moment, it was evident that there was in existence a no-man's land between two previously established camps; and that the time and opportunity appeared to have arrived to populate this no-man's land, and so to abolish the distinction established by the existence of the two camps. This concept was expressed by Charles Davis when he left the Roman Catholic Church:

'The Christian presence doesn't need a single grouping', he stated before leaving to take up a teaching post in Canada: 'it should be multiple, relative, changing. The Christian life needs an all-embracing setting, not an organisation but the world itself.'

One further point must be made, before taking up the chronological account of the non-church movement. Many letters I received were from church-going parents whose children had no desire to be associated with any church, yet were, in many cases, young people with a strong social sense, and desperately anxious to serve the community. Nina Borelli, in a famous article in *Christian Comment* entitled 'Some hard facts about Christian Youth Work' outlined something of the dilemma faced by such young people:

> Two or three years ago the Christian Youth Committee of the British Council of Churches Youth Department were asked what they thought was the most difficult thing they did as young Christians. A young Congregationalist girl answered that she believed that no greater iron curtain existed than that between the young people inside the Church and the young people outside. They lived in the same society, they worked in the same place, they travelled on the same buses, they went to the same schools, they looked exactly alike. But at the moment they went to Church on Sunday they became segregated, not just separated, from their own contemporaries; and they now found this an unbridgeable gap. . . . *We* have become the segregated society. . . . Often a Church has to abandon its premises and go out to where young people are, not as commando teams or hot gospellers, but in order to listen to the questions young people ask, in the places where they are at ease.[4]

My own experience of teaching in a technical college for nearly ten years convinces me that the rising generation has largely rejected organized religion. The few who acknowledge religious belief usually belong to the more exclusive sects, and, incidentally, have virtually no contribution to make in the field of liberal studies which I teach. It was the evidence provided by this generation which led me years ago to the conclusion that the Church could not survive beyond another generation, except in the form of tiny pockets of exclusivism. Not one shred of evidence has been produced from any source to suggest that this is other than a realistic appraisal of the situation. The whole matter was made more challenging to me by the fact that it was manifestly not an unwillingness to be *committed* to any body which prevented the young from attending church: their loyalty to the

Beatles, and to certain ideas propagated by these remarkable young men, disproved that; the task for people of my generation was to express some concept related to human values to which the rising generation could respond with enthusiasm. The question was whether in the non-church concept lay the seed which could provide the answer.

The response to my initial articles, numerically and in terms of the groups of people represented, was wide enough to justify following up the suggestion made by many of the writers: that a conference should be convened in order for people to meet and find out together whether there was any future in the concept of 'non-church'. The then Bishop of Woolwich, John Robinson, had already booked a centre for a conference on the theme of his book *Honest to God.* With the kindness and generosity typical of the man, he offered me this centre, for January 1967, expressing a willingness to attend as one of the participants. I accepted this offer with considerable gratitude, even though the centre at Bletchingley could accommodate only thirty, when five times that number were to express a desire to attend.

The conference was unique in my experience. It was described by one participant, Michael De La Noy, in a report he wrote as 'almost a non-conference'.[5] This was probably because, unlike most conferences, we had no programme. As chairman, my aim was solely to keep the discussion moving, with group discussion alternating frequently, throughout the two days, with plenary reports and decisions about what next should be tackled in the groups. The only positive outcome which I was determined should ensue was a statement of sorts outlining an answer to the question, 'Where do we go from here?' Here is how one participant, Jeremy Goring, summed up the conference in general:

On a wintry weekend in January 1967 thirty-five people, for the most part strangers to each other, came together for a conference in a large country house in Surrey. They came from all over England, and from a wide variety of religious backgrounds: Roman Catholic, Anglican, Methodist, Unitarian, Jewish, Agnostic, Humanist. Some were active in churches; others had severed all ecclesiastical connections. Some were trained theologians; others had made no systematic study of religion. But in spite of these differences there emerged a remarkable unanimity of spirit. As the weekend wore on and the level of talk deepened, so the theological ice-barriers melted and the denominational labels were forgotten. Persons related directly to persons, and a real community of the spirit came into being. At the close of the conference the gathering dispersed and people went their very different ways. 'We must meet again', they said. But that particular group will probably never reconvene. One cannot re-create a Pentecost.[6]

Despite the unanimity of spirit which we certainly experienced, there were major differences in emphasis among participants. Perhaps because the atmosphere was so cordial, these differences were no more than a slightly discordant reverberation in the background. But within a year they were to emerge in the forefront of our discussions.

On my own assessment of the assembled company, there were three main motivations represented. Firstly, there were those whose chief concern lay in church renewal; they believed that whatever new forms of action might be recommended by the conference, it must continue to be primarily through the agency of the Church. They were critical of the majority decision not to hold any kind of prayers, or Sunday worship – and privately celebrated the Eucharist. There was then the group, with whom at the time I identified myself, who were concerned simply with the issue already presented: how to create some form of communication between those just inside and those just outside the Church; none of these, whatever else in the Christian faith they might object to, took exception to being identified with the mission of Jesus as they personally interpreted it. Thirdly, there were those who affirmed that it would be unwise to nail the members down to any kind of theological language whatever, including the name Jesus. Their view was that language was deceptive and divisive, and that if we attempted to be too explicit we might thereby alienate people who, in all but the vocabulary they used, were in full agreement with others using theological vocabulary. This third group had in its number some of the most able advocates at the conference; I estimate that at the start the general opinion lay somewhere between the first and second groups: by the end, it had moved to between the second and third.

On the final afternoon, an agreed statement was produced which was later handed to the press. It read:

Many of us feel a dissatisfaction with the organized Church. However, we have found this conference to be a fruitful meeting ground for those who ask questions about our present situation. To provide further opportunities for such meetings, we are encouraging small 'non-church' groups to discuss reality and meaning in human life. Such groupings may evolve out of the interests of everyday life. But there seems to be a need to pursue these questions on new meeting grounds. These proposed groups would be open to all, whether or not they have any commitment to organized religion. In short, we seek a meeting ground for people who ask questions about reality and meaning in human life.

Perhaps this did not say very much, in which case this was not unlike official statements in other areas of life. However, it gave us the lead-in to the one practical step of the conference: to duplicate the names and addresses in areas of all who had written to me, and to send these out with a covering note emphasizing that establishing any contact between people in a particular area was their own responsibility. What they were to discuss, and the direction their discussions might take, were also their responsibility. There would be no office, no secretariat, and, above all, no high priest.

What kind of community?

Before outlining subsequent developments in the non-church movement, it is important to be explicit about its prime motivation. The radical experiment at Woolwich, and similar expressions of radicalism elsewhere, were church-centred and church-approved, at least initially. (It is significant that official approval diminished as the centre of gravity shifted.) An inevitable corollary of such experiments is that the Church looks for 'results' which can be tabulated and used in evidence for or against the particular experiment. It would be foolish to expect otherwise. The Church is a visible community, a number of organisms separated from the rest of society by various tests of membership. There are those who are 'in' and those who are 'out', and consequently anything undertaken 'outside' must be able to justify itself by increased numbers 'inside'. One report of the Home Missions Department of the Methodist Church stated this clearly:

We believe that the Church is God's creation, that he has called it to be 'the people of God', 'his servants to the world'. There can be no penetration of the world without a base from which to work. That base is and must be the living Church. There can be no 'Go' structure without a 'Come' structure.[7]

So we find that where churches have participated in liturgical experiments, it has been necessary to report on the numbers of new, particularly young, people who have attended as a result. House churches, lay training centres, churches with coffee bars, have all been reported on as bringing 'outsiders' into the orbit of church life. Team ministries have had to face the questions: what are you doing more than others? What have you to show for all this concentrated manpower? For example, the lack of confirmation candidates at St. Mary's brought us a question from the Bishop of Southwark: why were we not pressurizing people more in this direction?

What must be acknowledged is that if increased attendances at Church are to be the test of the worth of any experiments undertaken, these must be adjudged to have failed. As David Gourlay stated in *The Guardian*:

> I sometimes think that the intelligent and discerning just laugh at Christian mental gymnastics to prove that they are 'with it' and really open to change. All manner of refreshing and exciting ventures are taking place in almost every branch of the Church today. But why is the world – if we can use so vague and ambiguous a term – not more impressed?[8]

He then proceeded to challenge the basic supposition underlying these experiments in the minds of church hierarchies:

> More and more it seems we must realize that living for others may not necessarily entail bringing them into the orbit of organized religion at all. The Christian does not take religion to the man next door or to the person with problems. He tries to 'be for the other' in and through all the dangers and contradictions of such a relationship.

In other words, what is required is not so much experiment as exploration. An experimenter, by definition, has some idea, within certain definable limits, of what he will experience. He works and thinks deductively, beginning with a general, unchallenged, concept, which he proceeds to test in a particular situation. His findings here may well require a change in the definition of the original concept, but the whole process is circumscribed and comparatively 'closed'. The explorer, on the other hand, thinks and acts inductively. He has a particular idea in mind, but has no idea what general concept or system of beliefs this will lead him to. Like the physical explorer, the explorer in the realm of ideas proceeds without any certainty of what he will find at the end of the trail. So far as the Christian explorer is concerned, this means, in the words of Peter Berger:

> Christians . . . must relinquish the idea that, in inviting both Christians and non-Christians to communication (dialogue) they will subject the latter to some subtle religious manipulation. They must not merely say, but honestly realize themselves, that they cannot know the answers to most of the problems arising in the dialogue. They must abandon the rhetorics of moral authority which too many contemporaries have learned to recognize as empty and pretentious verbiage. . . . This posture has been called that of the listening Church.[9]

In short, this means taking 'secular' society seriously, valuing it for itself rather than as a company of people to be pressurized. To be more basic, it means discarding altogether the 'us' and 'them' mentality.

This point was raised in relation to the concept of the Christian community by the then Bishop of Woolwich at the conference at Bletchingley. (He was too ill to attend in person, but sent us a tape-recorded address, which was later published in *New Christian*.[10]) He began by quoting from Malcolm Boyd's *Free to Live, Free to Die* (condensed from the evening meditation of the Twenty-first Day):

> It used to be easier to speak of community. In fact in-groups were even accepted as a part of life which wasn't questioned. Community was understood in terms of *this* group, or *that* one . . .
>
> But now, community has more complex meanings. Most people have come to realize that community isn't a *place* but a state of being, fluid and ongoing, marked less by a post-office address than an attitude shared by persons.
>
> Maybe the real secret of community now is that no one can arbitrarily be excluded. A so-called believer . . . doesn't want to be shut off from so-called unbelievers. . . . Whether one is speaking of fulfilment, salvation, or joy, no one wants it on a private preserve, shut off from others. Persons are claiming each other. Walls are coming *down*. A person is a sign-post to another.
>
> We are beginning to see that no one makes a community; he accepts community where and as it *is*.[11]

Dr. Robinson then proceeded to relate this concept to the Church:

'It is concerned with responding to community, accepting the responsibility of community, where it is, in the world, rather than organizing a community over against the world. I believe that this concern may be much closer to the New Testament than our inherited presuppositions have allowed us to see. . . .

It is noteworthy that the Church is never described in the New Testament as 'a community'. *Koinonia* is not a group of persons but a quality of relationship, a sharing, a participation. . . . The phrase 'the fellowship of the Holy Spirit' refers to participation in this divine reality, not in the first instance to fellowship between Christians (though that of course must follow), let alone to *the* fellowship of Christians. The Church is meant to be the embodiment, the carrier, the incarnation of the *koinonia* of Holy Spirit, as it is of the grace of our Lord Jesus Christ and of the love of God. But it is not a fellowship as such (any more than it is a love or a grace). . . .

To accept community where and as it *is*, is, in Christian terms, to respond to the presence of the Kingdom wherever it meets one, in the midst of life, wherever two or three are gathered. *Koinonia* is, theologically, the equivalent of the Kingdom, not of the Church. . . .

Church, or *ekklesia*, is in origin an Old Testament idea, and it means those who are 'called out'. It designates those who respond to the summons 'Come out from among them' to be a separated people, representative of the sacred as opposed to the secular, the holy as opposed to the common. But the great fact of the New Age, the *koinonia hagion*, (Holy community, holy communion) represents the making common of the holy – and therefore the end of the Church as a peculiar people. . . .

This frontier (between 'believers' and 'unbelievers') is likely to become increasingly irrelevant, and already the question of whether one is an 'insider' or an 'outsider' has ceased for many to be the significant one it was.

I have quoted at some length from this statement, since it puts the matter lucidly and succinctly. I don't know whether everybody at the conference was totally convinced by the argument, but the majority went away resolved to pursue this line of thinking, and to act upon it.

How far were we able to establish 'non-church groups' as indicated in our report? I deliberately did no more than send out the lists of addresses, so that I was never certain how many people were meeting, and what they were discussing. I heard from time to time of upwards of a dozen groups of varying sizes who were making the act of exploration for themselves. Some of these continue to meet, and I hear from them occasionally. My own experience, however, typifies that of many at the conference and among the correspondents: I found enough opportunity to pursue the areas of enquiry suggested in our report at my own sphere of work in a technical college – with students, of course, but even more pertinently among my colleagues – without feeling the need to convene an extra ad hoc meeting. Indeed, I might say that over the period under discussion I found that the need to be constantly meeting with people outside working hours – as happens in the majority of churches – had almost entirely disappeared. Perhaps the fortnightly (as it had by then become) staff meeting at St. Mary's provided all I needed psychologically in group discussion; certainly over the next three years the hankering after meetings became less and less intense, until now (in 1970) I attend virtually none at all. Occasionally the prospect of an evening meeting seems suddenly to have its merits; but this is now more a sense of nostalgia for the past than a real need perceived in the present.

However, as I have stated, I am fortunate in working within a situation in which not all talk is 'shop' talk, and when a social evening with colleagues can become one of intense creative discussion together. In addition, I have the added advantage that application of some of the ideas which are thrashed out can be made in the daily situation. As I shall be arguing later, the sphere of education seems to be the chief area in which the battle for man's future independence and maturity will be fought; so I am, in my own estimation, in the human 'front line' in any case. But what about those who are not: those who either don't go out to work and consequently have few natural opportunities for such discussion, or, in their work, find that such opportunities either do not naturally accrue or, if accruing, are not generally taken up by their colleagues except as opportunities for casual conversation? One of the needs expressed at the conference was for the opportunity of people to *declare* their secularity – to indicate by their words and behaviour that they are no longer committed to a church-based, church-dominated perspective for living. Many of them had left the Church in which they had been office-bearers, and often the criticisms from behind had been intensified for them by a sense of loneliness in the kind of no-man's land in which they felt themselves to have arrived. Simply to know that others in their neighbourhood were exploring like themselves could give strength and courage.

Objections

Before outlining what has occurred in relation to non-church since the Bletchingley conference, I shall consider some of the criticisms which were made of the movement during the period that followed.

(a) *This new form of radicalism is simply 'old' liberalism in a new guise.*

If this criticism were true, I suppose those who welcomed the concept of non-church would find their natural habitat in the Modern Churchmen's Union. But there are two basic differences between the two. Firstly, however critical liberals may be towards the Church, they remain basically reformers and renewers rather than transplanters and revolutionaries. To them, however decadent or corrupt the Church may be, its permanency is not questioned. Our view, on the contrary, was that the Church by its very existence as a separate organism could never unite men in a common understanding of the meaning of life, and a common sharing of the abundant life, as proclaimed by Jesus. In order to discover afresh what he and his message meant for mankind, it was essential to withdraw from the Church which imprisoned and shrouded him in the strait-jacket of creed and dogma.

This does not mean, however, that we were anxious to write our brand of theology; and here the second distinction between non-church and liberalism emerges. The tendency among liberals is to see Jesus as a great teacher, and they consequently view their prime task as that of extracting from the Creeds those elements which throw this teaching into relief, so that men can recognize its basic commonsense. 'Love' is the key word in their vocabulary, and 'the enthronement of love as revealed in Jesus' their motive for living. Obviously, this is elemental as a motive for human relationships, but the liberals appear to lack a sense of realism insofar as they affirm that, provided love is the motive, the way will be clear in every situation. They ignore the reality of the power structure in politics; they seem blind to the tensions which afflict people, especially contemporary young people:

62

the nature of authority, of freedom, and personal discipline and responsibility in the allegedly permissive society which has evolved. The liberals, by extracting one element (albeit a crucial one) from the life and teaching of Jesus, seem to bear in mind distorted pictures of contemporary human situations, so that the answers they present are non-answers because, high-sounding and commendable though they may be, they are not applicable since they do not fit the existing terms of reference.

The non-church was motivated from the start by the ideal of 'freedom to be', and this distinguishes it from all shades of religious liberalism. We were not simply a group of people tired of the restriction and impositions of the Church, seeking to commune with God through nature or whatever, and aiming solely at being kind to all men. We were a group of people disenchanted with the 'isms' of our upbringing, and looking for the best way of applying our varied energies and insights unitedly within the human situation. Because of this, no label yet devised by man could adequately describe us.

(b) *If the truths embodied in the concept of non-church are to be widely disseminated, some form of organization will be essential. In the course of time this will stabilize itself and be 'established' so that in the end it would be a breakaway movement and, inasmuch as its members include former church-attached people, schismatic.*

The aim behind non-church included the widening of people's horizons; if, therefore, it could be demonstrated that we had succeeded only in creating a new, enclosed structure, this would certainly be a powerful argument against the viability of our enterprise. Experience over three years (long enough by modern standards of development and progress) suggests that neither opponents nor supporters of non-church have any cause for alarm. Our only organization remains a list of names and addresses, and local convenors who make themselves responsible for arranging meetings. There is no united action between groups, no concerted policy. There is as yet no non-church representative on the World Council of Churches. There is no hierarchy, and no annual conference. The only structure, if we may use that over-employed word, is the community within which the people concerned are placed.

Some of the participants, as a matter of fact, continue to attend their local churches; others include men and women who never were inside a church, besides those who feel compelled to cease their erstwhile church-attending practices. I cannot speak for all participants, but my own impression is that the harshest words about the Church today are being spoken by the renewers 'within', rather than by non-church 'without' (if these topographical allusions have any meaning still). The general view in non-church is that if people continue to be helped by church attendance in their own personal quests, it would be presumptuous of us to criticize. Meanwhile, our own personal acts of exploration have brought us together in this way (and this book is an outline of the ideas to which this exploration has led at least one participant).

To those who prefer to have matters, and people, cut-and-dried so that they can be easily card-indexed and filed away, this situation will appear unsatisfactory, if not schizophrenic. I prefer to describe it as an example of what Dr. Robinson calls 'an age of overlap'.[12] If it is true that man has reached a new stage in his destiny, as some assert[13] we can hardly be criticized for wanting to divine which way the next stage will go, and possibly to play a part in shaping it. The very fact that the Church *per se* belongs to the old order precludes it from playing a positive role in this: most churchmen will probably express contempt for any suggestion about a new evolutionary phase. Those of us who yet wish to speak and act in relation to our environment – the human situation, which includes, but is not dependent on, the Church – require wider perspectives than this one segment of society can offer. We wish not only to be men of this age, but to be heard and seen to be so; and if this brings us the charge of being schismatics, we can bear this with equanimity: there are, after all, other ways of looking at life than that proclaimed by, and represented in, the Church.

I accept the strength of Howard Williams' argument[14] that incarnation is written into any 'religious' practice whether this word be interpreted in the narrow sense of belief in the supernatural, or the broad sense of concern about people. That is, I acknowledge that, while a vision remaining untranslated into practical reality can maintain itself pure and unsullied, once this translation occurs, the tensions and mixed motives, the confusion and strife associated with all human affairs, are bound to be involved. But the risks involved can be accepted: what will emerge after ten or twenty years cannot possibly be foretold at this stage. Meanwhile, in the words of the politicians, our aim is to keep all our options open. The weakness of being church-directed is that it curtails the number of options.

(c) *Those who act independently of the church neglect the claims of history.*

This criticism assumes what was accepted above about the nature of religious activity. Howard Williams expresses the objection in these words:

> Nothing will be gained by uprooting a growth for which we have no right to feel shame. The fundamental point here is that you cannot ignore roots, just as the Christian faith will grow thin if it tries to forsake Israel.[15]

Obviously, any man would be a fool if he imagined that he could divorce himself from history and environment. In fact 'fool' is hardly a strong enough term. Peer Gynt said of those in his mental asylum:

> It's here that men are most themselves – themselves and nothing but themselves – sailing with outspread sails of self. Each shuts himself in a cask of self, the cask stopped in a bung of self and seasoned in a well of self. None has a tear for others' woes or cares what any other thinks.

It is because those in the non-church care intensely what others think that they have made the response which I have described; and it is because they do not wish to be circumscribed about whom they shall listen to that they desire to meet in a wider context than that of either the Church or any other organization with which they may have been associated. Gordon Rupp warns us that many of the so-called radicals speak too highly of the secular city to the point of romanticising it:

> If the man in the street has his honesties and insights, he has his errors also.[16]

Of course he has: if it were not so those inside would long ago have capitulated to those outside the Church.

Defenders of the historical perspective beg the question of how we, or any others engaged in similar activity, were doing despite to history. It is assumed that to write off doctrines, absolutes, dogmas, of the past as too limiting in the present is to repudiate the claims of history. In fact, there are many in non-church who accept the claims, for instance, of the Christian creeds, and wish simply to find a new setting for these which will make them available to all men rather than for the select few. Even those who reject the claims acknowledge, and know that they can never escape from, both the influence of doctrines on their past, and their effect, sub-consciously, on present ideas and practices. There was a good deal of the Pharisee in St Paul right up to the end. A man's upbringing, and the influences which shaped it, cannot be eradicated.

But perhaps this is treating the criticism on a personal level, when it was intended in terms of movements or organizations. Here again, any objective observer at Bletchingley would have commented on the extent to which most of us were the offspring, however illegitimate, of the Church. Eventually, perhaps, others will be seen as emerging from the humanist, Jewish, or Marxist camps. These are all historically inter-related, and therefore share a common interdependence. Our indebtedness is to all these. But just as Christianity emerged from Judaism, and Islam and Marxism from the Christian-Judaic syndrome, so it appears that the time is ripe for a new emergence, more dramatic than these others since it will embody strands from a wide range of historical 'isms'. To say that this would be more revolutionary than any earlier development is simply to acknowledge what has already been claimed: that we are on the threshold of a totally new step forward in human destiny. But even *that* claim is not new, and it is probably not the last time it will be made.

The evidence for this claim, and an approach to the content of any answer to the challenge it represents, will be the theme of the final section. It can be stated now that to make the claim is not to ignore the violence of our age, the cruelty, the indifference, the megalomania. There are obvious pitfalls ahead and the possibility exists that man's next dramatic step will be that of annihilating himself. But the existence of the hydrogen bomb and other weapons of mass destruction has forced man to think internationally; it has produced a vision of world community; and if the discoveries of science and technology, and the insights of sociology and psychology, as well as those of religion, can be made available to all men, then a new golden age promises the human race.

Some have spoken of our age as 'a new Reformation'. I prefer to think of it as a new Renaissance, in which many of the received ideas of our generation must go into the melting pot. Far from divorcing themselves from the historical process, therefore, those who pursued the concept of non-church believed themselves to be moving with the tide of history. It seems to me beyond dispute that if man's destiny on this planet is to fulfil the dreams of the optimists and not confirm the despair of the pessimists and cater for the blindness and cowardice of the indifferent, some commit-

66

ment to a new cause, a faith, if you like, in human possibilities, is required on the part of any who are not so far embedded in the groove in which they were reared that they are incapable of breaking out into fresh terrain.

From the historical point of view, the Church as a potent influence on mankind has already ceased to be – has done so since the early part of this century. But like Judaism before it, it is likely to pursue its channelled course for the sake of the few to whom it appeals. For the rest, it will remain as a sign of the rock from which many of us, and many of our ideas, were hewn; and, by the same token, of the cul-de-sac which future generations need not explore. If what it proclaimed has any universal validity, then the proclamation must be released from the narrow interpretation which, inevitably, the Church has been compelled to give it. If Jesus was, as I believe, *the* free man of history, then it remains a tragic irony that hitherto the meaning and the message of the man have been restricted largely to a narrowly ecclesiastical interpretation.

(d) *Can we be sure that, without the Church as custodians, the message would survive among future generations? The 'machine' which we condemn has ensured the continued teaching of the Christian faith through the centuries; could we provide alternative means of doing this?*

The answer here depends on how far it is desired that the teaching of orthodox Christianity should continue. There are those in the non-church movement who feel that it must; others are quite indifferent about it. The difference in emphasis was, as I shall shortly explain, to cause a major division between us at the ensuing conference. Clearly, those desirous of its continuing would be mainly those who, though attending non-church groups occasionally, continued also to attend church.

For those who had no interest in the continuing presentation of the received faith, the image of a future without, for instance, compulsory R.I. in every British school, or of church buildings closing until their existence became a rare phenomenon, held no alarms. The absolutes of one generation can be, in any case, the relatives of the next. All that can honestly be taught to any new generation is the ideas which have motivated the human race until then: after that, from then on, if this new generation has accepted its birthright and begun to stand on its own feet, they must go ahead and work out their own approach to living – what is good, and true, and of value. The signposts they encounter can only indicate the direction from which they have come; only they can discover what to write on the shield pointing ahead. For there are no absolute values, no ultimate truths; and there is no unique faith. We shall have served future generations if our energies have been directed towards encouraging men and women, the crown of creation, to think creatively. Men cannot go on for ever being contented sheep, letting others do the worrying and planning for them: they must become suffering gods, as Lewis Mumford remarked, aware of and sharing the tensions and trials of humanity. As we shall see, it was along these lines, or something akin to these, that one element in non-church began eventually to move.

I know that my views have disturbed some of those who remain in the Church. So, lest I be identified with the 'young turks' who seem bent on shaking the organization to pieces, I will conclude this consideration of objections to the idea of non-church, all of which have emanated from church circles, with a quotation from Peter Berger which is the nearest statement to my own position that I have so far found:

> As far as the local congregation is concerned, our considerations lead us to a somewhat paradoxical conclusion. We find ourselves far more radical than most in negatively estimating the potentialities of the institution. At the same time, we would be more conservative than most in terms of what we would want to do with the institution. The clue to the paradox, of course, is our contention that the most urgent tasks before us can be dealt with outside the institution and, at least in certain cases, with little reference to it. The local congregation can then be left to what it has always done and perhaps will always do in the future – liturgy, preaching, the administration of the sacraments, and whatever educational activities seem plausible to those concerned. Essential tasks of the Christian Mission in our society can then be undertaken (radically if need be) outside the local congregation.[17]

There remain within the Church those who still find strength and encouragement from traditional activities and expressions of belief. These should be left to work together, while those whose convictions take them in a different direction find their own 'scene'. If what I have been arguing in this section is right, that the words 'outside' and 'inside' are no longer indicative of the stark divisiveness which previous generations maintained, then most of those who go out to explore do so in the assurance that some, at least, of those they have left behind wish them well. In this age of overlap we need have no books with the theme of 'I leap over the wall': the walls are down, and if some still prefer to remain within the battlements, this does not stop others from stepping with ease over the dividing lines which remain only as historical signs in the ground. I describe myself as a 'Christian outsider', not 'the enemy within'.

Later developments

As with the section on the Woolwich experiment, the last part of this section will relate chiefly how matters and ideas have developed so far as I am personally concerned. Others have certainly followed a similar course, but we have not, as yet, consciously done so together.

In November 1967, it was felt by several of us that a further, one-day, conference was advisable, since we had received many more letters of enquiry during the intervening ten months. The meeting was arranged to be held in London in December, and the following letter was sent to several newspapers:

> Anyone today who is concerned with such issues as war, poverty, race and human values must be aware that traditional systems of thought and social organization are failing to cope with them.
>
> The young especially distrust traditional knowledge and culture. Many insist on debunking the old while reaching for the new.
>
> For the past year a number of small groups have been meeting to consider what values and symbols (if any) are worth preserving for the future. We wholeheartedly applaud the current dissatisfaction with past systems – whether religious or philosophical, political or economic, social or educational.
>
> We have called our groups 'non-church' because our particular disenchantment has been with organized religion in this country. But we would like to meet others who care about the quality of modern life and the values and symbols which may help to make it meaningful.

Attendance at this conference was restricted to about seventy by the occurrence of a nation-wide freeze-up, which prevented almost that number from joining us from outside London. In the event, the refrigeration without threw into relief the combustion within.

The main issue which I presented to the members of the conference had been put to me as a crucial problem by two of the non-church groups: granted that meetings were not held with the purpose of belabouring the cause of church reform, how far should those with a church background remain committed to religious language? Were they in any way being disloyal to their faith if they attempted to express the motives for their exploration in purely human terms? If religious terms were a stumbling-block in any encounter with 'non-religious' people (in the sense that these were not committed to any belief in what may loosely be described as the 'supernatural') was it not preferable, in the interests of communication between the two, that they should be dropped? Or should the situation be viewed as part of the cross which has to be borne by any contemporary Christian explorer, because of the image he inherits from a Church which, both in its practices and in its presentation of doctrines, appears to many to have moved a long way from the mind and message of its founder?

In short, were words like 'God', 'Jesus Christ', 'Holy Spirit', 'sin', 'faith', or 'salvation' to be discarded because they might add confusion to a dialogue, or to be deliberately introduced and, where necessary, re-interpreted so as to demonstrate that the differences between, say, Christians and humanists were apparent only when discussion remained on a theoretical level but largely disappeared when they were expressed in terms of human motivation, behaviour, and action?

As at the previous conference, three main viewpoints emerged during the course of the day. Firstly, there were those, intensely radical though they manifestly were, who felt that to lay aside their religious beliefs, for whatever motive, would represent a betrayal of themselves and the position they held. As one delegate expressed it, if Jesus Christ *is* the Son of God, then no amount of rethinking, demythologizing, call it what you will, can alter the fact that he is unique; he epitomizes the answer to the world's need, and to sacrifice this truth would be to remove the one sure guiding light within the darkness of the human dilemma. While not wishing to be committed to the methods whereby the Church proclaimed him, therefore, those holding this view remained convinced that the name Jesus Christ could not be set aside in any discussion about the human condition.

At the other extreme were a small group who either had never held beliefs about, for instance, Jesus, as proclaimed by the Church, or, having held these beliefs at one time, had come to reject them. This group felt that any introduction of religious doctrine into whatever discussions were to ensue would be to remove those discussions from the main area in which they should be involved – the practical problems resulting from the abiding issue, how shall men live? Whatever the presuppositions on which action was based, concepts must ultimately express themselves empirically; consequently, it seemed to this group that for others to insist on raising issues of theology would be to divert them from their main course. Among those who held this view were several who were anxious to see 'non-church' aligning itself with the new left, and participating in the attempt to express some kind of 'political theology' unhampered by any current political theory.

Between these groups were those who took a *via media*, and with whom at the time I associated myself. Our view was that Christian theology and religious practice could not, if they were true to themselves, exist in a vacuum. The test of doctrine and of churchmanship was how these affected people's private and corporate decisions and actions. As a matter of fact, many decisions reached by Christians were along the same lines as those arrived at by people holding no religious views and practising no brand of churchmanship. The basis on which decisions were reached should, therefore, be viewed as a private matter; the public issue, the tangible element evinced in the choice of procedure (existentially) necessitated, was the only matter of ultimate concern. The traditional argument of Christians *vis-à-vis* humanists was that the latters' exemplifying of what some Christians would term Christian morality resulted from their having been reared in a society impregnated with Christian influences. We in our group discussions acknowledged that this was a presumptuous claim to make, and that it could be just as logically argued in reverse – that some Christians, despite the shocking example shown by many of their forebears, had 'caught' the prevailing spirit of humanity, humaneness, evinced by a society which was gradually following the evolutionary process from the jungle to a cultured existence.

I think that the emergence of these diverging approaches to the problem confronting us helped to clarify for some members where their real concern lay. Certainly a number of those who took the first of the three viewpoints left with some asperity, and it was clear that for them a radical renewal of Christianity and the Church was what they were primarily committed to. Those who took the middle line, many of whom were already meeting in non-church groups, felt that this conference had confirmed them in their current procedure, and continue to meet. At the other wing, those who did not accept, or were indifferent to, either religious or any other kind of doctrine as indicated in the invitatory letter, resolved to go ahead and meet solely on that basis. They wanted to explore how far modern novelists, painters and psychologists had any insights to present about the human condition, and whether there was any possibility of starting to enunciate the meaning and purpose of existence in terms which did not depend for their efficacy on any kind of inherited moral, religious, political or philosophical concepts. This group named itself the 'Four Winds' group, and continues to meet. At this stage, however, my own writings and contacts brought the non-church movement as I understood it to a much broader basis, and I must now outline developments over the ensuing two years.

So far as I personally was concerned, a certain crystallization of thinking evinced itself in two articles, one in *New Christian* in May 1968, and one in *The Guardian* the following August. The former was given the title 'The Tedious Church Reformers', and in it I parted company with the radicals of the Church who yet concluded that their place, and main sphere of operation, lay inside the church structure rather than outside. I suggested that religion and its attendant activities had for these people become a drug from which, however hard they tried, they could not free themselves. I expressed astonishment that Colin Morris, in his book *Include Me Out!* should even imagine that an ecclesiastical organization could, by its nature, have priorities other than ecclesiastical. I stated my own disinterest in the question of the Church's survival since it was to be doubted whether Jesus had ever intended that such an organization should come into existence in any case. It seemed fairly obvious to me that the matters of primary concern within the Church were trivial compared with the – as it seemed – weightiest contemporary issue: how shall men live? The *fact* that most people today rejected church affiliation had certainly been noted by some of those inside it; few of them had perceived why this was so: that most people today simply did not accept the – to use a shorthand term – supernatural foundation on which the ecclesiastical edifice was built.

This led to the crucial question with which we had been

grappling in non-church: does the Christian attempt to restate his beliefs in terms that communicate directly to the experience and understanding of non-christians? The Bishop of Woolwich (as he then was) had attempted to do this in *Honest to God*, but I felt that the attempt to restate 'God' in contemporary psychological terms was doomed to failure since, having rejected the Person who 'has made us for Himself' one arrives at a new – or, at least, different – concept, for which new language emerging from different premises was required. In other words, I suggested, the time had come to discard altogether the symbols and myths inherited from earlier generations. 'We must work and think from the ground up, not from heaven down.'

I defended this idea against the charge of being nothing more than humanism on the grounds that humanism itself presented man with 'received' tenets, and that I had no more desire to be stamped with their image than with that of the Church. What I was convinced was necessary was 'for all those people – and they will be primarily young people – whose attitude to received systems is a simple 'plague on all your houses' – including the disenchanted members of these different houses – to come together in order to think and work creatively, to construct out of our present impasse an expression of human values which will tackle the major problems of our time, and will enable more men everywhere to discover the infinite depths and ecstatic heights of human nature.' I suggested briefly how a beginning in this direction might be made, and concluded by facing the criticism that in suggesting this course I was breaking faith with those who had turned to non-church primarily in order to rediscover life in terms of Christ, but untrammelled by ecclesiasticism. To these I said:

> First, I feel that Jesus, although naturally restricted by concepts relevant to his own age, was essentially working in this direction. His words about abundant life were geared to the present, and, 'demythologized', amount to an affirmation of human values. But, secondly, it would be a paradoxical denial of this if at every turn we were committed to the invocation of his name. So long as we do this, we shall be restricted by the myths and images which have been attached to it through the centuries. If we are to discover what were his basic concerns, we shall do so only by refusing to make him into a God.

This article was naturally received with something less than fervour by *New Christian* readers. One reader angrily rejected what she described as 'thinly disguised humanism'; another stated that man was incapable of the kind of creative activity I advocated. Anthony Wesson wrote a detailed criticism. He disagreed with my analysis of the present situation regarding belief in God and suggested that since it was notoriously difficult to define a human being in the first place, my advocacy of 'the unity of the species' as a starting-point for a statement of human values was question-begging. He suspected that I was at heart a manichee, interested only in individual acts without reference to community. The problems facing men, he suggested, were not only how they were to live, but where they could find the resources to love. Both Church and non-church appeared to be equally perplexed about the answer to this. Finally, Douglas Rhymes argued that in his experience young people were in most matters as reactionary as their parents, and most people simply did not want to think and work creatively, or to consider the major problems of their time.

My own reaction to these criticisms was twofold. I recognized that my article used emotive words – like 'parasites' in reference to contemporary attitudes to parsons – which could perhaps provide heat in the mind of any reader, but little light. I had laid myself open to the comment,

> He only does it to annoy
> Because he knows it teases.

In other words, I had been guilty of the very offence for which I was berating the radicals – only infuriating those whom it was hoped would be influenced.

This led to the further consideration: why had this emotive language crept in? My conclusion was that unconsciously I was in the process of realizing that the ideas which I was propounding would not, or could not at that time, be taken up by those in the Church situation, however sympathetic they might be to the particular views. In other words, whereas at the start some of those who met in non-church groups still continued to attend church, it would be difficult if not impossible for them to do so if they were to lay aside any kind of religious language. The only possible conclusion from this was that, for the time being at least, the direction of my main appeal would have to be away from, rather than towards, the Church. This meant that I had perhaps underestimated the height of the barrier dividing the 'Christian' from the 'non-Christian'. So long as any person desired to bear the label 'Christian' he was automatically committing himself to certain affirmations about a person, Christ, and he could only repudiate this by rejecting the label. And to take this last step, while it would not necessarily cause his exclusion from the Christian fold, would certainly make uncomfortable any time he spent in liturgical and ecclesiastical activity.

This consideration compelled me to examine my own beliefs more carefully; and I expressed these in the *Guardian* article, 'Bringing Down the Mighty'. I stated that for many people the problem about attending church was not that they disliked, for instance, antiquated versions of the *Magnificat* but that they could not understand who was the 'He' who had 'brought down the mighty from their seats'. I shall quote the remainder of this article *in toto*, since it raises issues which will be of primary concern throughout the rest of this book.

A few of those involved in church reform have realized this, and have begun to express their views in relation to a wider context. This is, to find 'Christ' at work in the various facets of life – in life's joys and sorrows, its cares and problems; in human relationships and the tensions which arise from these; and in the continuous process of an evolving society, with its birth pangs and death-knells. 'Jesus our Contemporary' and 'The Secular Christ' become the accepted phrases, and there is no denying that among the protagonists of this outlook are to be found most of the genuine radicals (as opposed to tidiers-up) in the Church. But what they apparently fail to realize (or, at least, do not acknowledge) is that *their* expression of 'Christ' is, like all people's expressions, subjective. In other words, it helps them in their thinking; the question is, does it help others?

I personally doubt it, for the same reason that I doubt the usefulness of any theological language – 'God', or 'faith' or 'sin' or any other 'great' New Testament word. The fact is that in attempting to communicate with people without biblical or theological training, and without any church background, the word 'Jesus' or 'Christ' is a hindrance to understanding. However hard I may try to show in general discussion that I am not tied down to the dogmas of the Church, once I have brought up this name I am pigeon-holed as a sheep in wolf's clothing – a Christian like other Christians, except that I am somewhat odder than most. The only way to find the communication I seek is to reject, and refuse to use – ever – the name Jesus in support of, or as having first proclaimed, the ideas I seek to express.

To those who hold that 'confession of the Name' is crucial to being termed a Christian, this must mean my exclusion from the fold. This seems somewhat ironical in the light of the attitude of Jesus, itself expressed in the Gospels. We see (or should I write only 'I see'?) one who refused to card-index people according to various laid-down standards, who was not in the slightest degree worried in what name people acted so long as they acted rightly, and whose whole ministry was aimed at man's achieving to the full the gift of his own humanity. Whether this interpretation be too subjective or not, it seems fairly clear that this is the fundamental need of our own time. And because this is so, there are certain implications which will inevitably be opposed by adherents of any fixed system of beliefs. I shall mention two of these implications.

The first is that man is no longer going to allow himself to be card-indexed, so that he can be described as a Christian, a humanist, a technocrat, or a Left/Right-winger. Any system of thought which simply tries to impose its concepts from 'above' (whether this be interpreted in a religious or historical sense) will be rejected. People are not blind today, and they have noticed that none of these systems, religious, political, sociological, or technical, have been able to solve the great problems of our time: race, poverty, war, class, nationalism.

The second follows from this. What is needed now is for all people, of whatever political, philosophical, or religious background, who see that all 'systems' have reached the end of the road, to meet in order to discover how best to express human values, and the meaning and purpose of life. New forms, perhaps new symbols, will need to be created; the aim will be how best to describe and experience human fulfilment. It will involve an affirmation that we are no longer to be described in any circumscribed way at all; we do not wish to be known as Christians, or Socialists, or humanists; we wish only to be known as human beings. This alone is the society to which we will belong.

Of course this is easier to write about than to achieve. If I understand him correctly, John Wilson at the Farmington Research Unit is finding that even to make the first tentative steps in this no-man's land is requiring the time and skills and insights of many people. It is perhaps the most difficult task facing the human race; it is certainly the most important, for if we cannot achieve a satisfactory understanding of life in solely human terms, one trembles to think what kind of absolutist thinking will be manipulating the human species within a few years.

This article, like its predecessor, was followed by a voluminous correspondence, both to *The Guardian* for publication, and to me personally. The published correspondence was given the reference 'The Church and Unlabelled Man', and of this latter Michael Lane wrote:

> Perhaps the Unlabelled Man could be recognized as one who, though he is committed to a variety of causes from time to time, refuses to give over-riding allegiance to any one organization, no matter what its pretensions, but only to the cause of undifferentiated humanity.

J. Hardie, writing from Aberdeen, said,

> Sri Ramakrishna, in the second half of the nineteenth century, likened the ritual and mythology of a religion to the husk, and the philosophy to a germ of a grain of rice. For too many centuries now, any form of spiritual progress has been baulked by the inherent dogma and esoteric nature of the ritual and mythological husks of religions, although the germs are identical.
>
> I suggest that the first step towards 'bringing down the mighty' should be by establishing the fact that such dogma need not exist, basing this on a definition of God as: 'Each human being's personal search for a truth to live by'.

The letters I personally received were, almost without exception, expressions of deep convictions along lines similar to those outlined in my article, and indicated that throughout the country a consensus of opinion is slowly growing with no explicit commitment to any traditional school of thought, yet 'religious' in the broadest sense of that word as involving profound concern about the human situation. I shall quote from just a handful of these, as typifying the attitudes expressed in nearly all of them.

> As you have said, people, especially young people, no longer accept the basic tenets of religious belief. It is difficult to say when this process started, but I would think certainly it has considerably accelerated during the last fifty years, owing

mainly to the spectacular and tremendous growth of scientific knowledge and attitudes of thinking. This has not only undermined, but in some areas completely destroyed, religious doctrine and has led to an acute inbalance in the mind of Man. It is a truism nowadays to say that our degree of control over the external world has not been matched by a corresponding understanding of the mind of Man and its mechanism, nor of the place of Man in the new and vastly extended universe which now confronts him. Such understanding is, I would suggest, a necessary prelude to any 'advance'. But whatever 'advance' is made in this particular direction, there would still be a need to tackle another problem. This is to my mind the necessity to synthesize Man's present knowledge, and how this can be done I cannot see at the moment, though the establishment of new natural laws and principles would appear to be a primary requirement for such a process to take place. These laws and principles must be embracing enough to encompass not only what is known of the physical world but also what is understood about the mind of Man.

I was thrilled to read your article and it was like meeting someone during an otherwise lonely journey.

This one was from a former Methodist local preacher:

I left, not because I thought the apparatus inappropriate or fast getting out of date (though I did think so), but because 'I doubt the usefulness of any theological language today'...

As a result of leaving, I am not forced into any system of thinking. I think and act more from the depth of myself which I trust. The result feels more like 'real religion'. The surface is formless, unmade by me, but underneath is the hidden order, the structure which has long been evolving in man. Most religion appears a panic reaction of the last few thousand years set against the slow evolution of deep strategies in the unconscious. 'We wish only to be known as human beings.'...

It is happening, a ferment beginning. Perhaps it is too early yet for too much conscious shaping, requiring at this stage a gentle stir rather than conscious effort with all its consequent pride, absolutism, and distortion.

A member of the British Humanist Association wrote:

As soon as the open secular society we envisage is achieved, then humanist, rationalist, secularist and other such organizations can quietly go out of business. And when tomorrow's schoolchildren read about us or learn from their teaching machines about the troubles we encountered, they will exclaim incredulously, 'But why did they have to be an organization, couldn't they all just BE human?' . . .

It is the slow wearing away of traditional authoritarianism, and the open discussion of these and allied matters which has created an atmosphere in which an article like yours can be accepted for publication. When I was seventeen, I couldn't even discuss it with my parents – let alone the Curate!

One writer, who found my article 'the most exciting since the time of the "Honest to God" stir', wrote:

Honest to God was the first theological book that ever really 'clicked' with me, after a period of unconscious restlessness with conventional Christianity. But after some time and further reading, it became apparent that although the Bishop asked the right questions and did useful demolition work, his constructive side was not really convincing, depending entirely on faith in a personal God. With the best will in the world I don't really understand what John Robinson means and cannot square his belief in worship etc. with the earlier part of the book. . . .

I can find no fault in most humanist statements except that they seem to be exclusively for the more intelligent and are very dull! Possibly what is required is a development of humanism but some 'life' is needed in that direction.

. . . Contemporary life in the western countries leans heavily on what is thought to be 'Christian' morality, and the collapse of the churches which now seems inevitable will leave society very exposed. . . .

It seems to me that you are trying to establish some post-Christian principles and I am very interested. Your article cheers me up to think that I am not the only person, unsatisfied with conventional religion, who sees the need for more than humanism.

Another correspondent took up the theme of man-without-labels:

I wonder if one part of the approach, or of the fundamental attitude, required in moving towards an anti-card-index frame of mind is to consider more fully, at any rate more consciously and continually, the likelihood of the element of chance in existence on earth: that one might just as well have been born in some other country, at some other time, of the other sex, even, perhaps, if one seeks a more embracing concept, as an animal (but where does one stop!)

If it is pure chance that one happens to be English, there is less to fuss about in the way of patriotism, racial superiority, and so on; similarly in terms of religion. (It has always seemed very unfair that people B.C. did not choose to pre-date Christ, or if A.D. had to be living in a very small catchment area to get an option on this new religion).

Another writer, a lady in Ipswich, was more interested in the problem of communication:

The first thing I want to say is that 'worship', which is how the orthodox still see 'the fundamental need', is becoming valueless to modern man, not so much because he fails to understand whom or what is being worshipped, but because 'worship' demands self-immolation and it is therefore a hindrance to his 'achieving to the full the gift of his own humanity'.

Your own expressions 'the communication I seek' and 'the ideas I seek to express' are much more likely, I think, to bring us to an understanding of the meaning and purpose of life. But I am wondering if there isn't first a big job to be done on ourselves by each one of us. Can we properly 'communicate' until we know ourselves? Religion, I think, is primarily a personal thing. If one cannot find the essential goodness in oneself, is one ever likely to experience it in communication with others?

And how can we engender this necessary self-knowledge? This is the big question! I am sure, from the tone of your article, you would not seek to bring it about by the evangelical efforts of a corps of élite. One is in the end forced to the view, I think, that the educational system should be slanted differently, giving more study to psychology, comparative religion, and the creative arts – particularly the last. Introspection – the examining of one's motives – should be encouraged rather than looked upon as unhealthy. If society became grounded in this more realistic, integrated attitude to life, then the communication you speak of would be natural and pleasurable.

Finally, here are some words of criticism written to me by a former colleague and friend in Taunton:

> You are an anarchist, almost a nihilist, and of course as such a necessary catalyst of today, when men are yearning, as seldom before, to be shown the way convincingly, to be shown a way, a path, shorn of all the weeds and hedges of old vocabularies and dogmas (half understood or not understood at all) which make it so difficult to see.
>
> But how circumscribed you are! 'We wish *only* to be known as human beings.' We have to 'achieve a satisfactory understanding of life in *solely* human terms'.
>
> Presumably we are to worship, if we are to worship anything, the whole human race or to aim at the whole human race's 'achieving to the full the gift of its humanity'. We are to dedicate ourselves to the world, to the human race, is that it? On the assumption that there is nothing more worthy of our dedication! We are perhaps to be like a good beehive where every bee lives, and if necessary dies, for the whole beehive? Or is that too fascist an idea? Or too communistic?
>
> You say that the *only* way to find the communication you seek is 'to reject, and refuse to use – ever – the name Jesus in support of, or as having first proclaimed, the ideas (you) seek to express'. Do you refuse to mention Plato or Gandhi or Buddha or Confucius or Bernard Shaw or Victor Gollancz or Graham Greene or Leibnitz or Lenin or Rolls-Royce or Henry Ford or Wilkinson Sword Blades or Che Guevara or Pasternak or Dostoevsky . . . ?
>
> Perhaps what is needed is a proscription of the Bible in any translation at all, thereby driving it underground, and perhaps a proscription of all texts in all other works mentioning any 'great' New Testament words. It would be fascinating to sit back and watch the results as the seeds began to germinate again from underground.

I suppose I invited the broadside in the penultimate paragraph here by my use of the absolute 'ever' in reference to use of the name of Jesus. Clearly, I am to a considerable extent dependent in my thinking on thoughts that have been expressed by men throughout history, before whom my own powers of thought are puny indeed. But it happens that, so far as western civilization generally is concerned, only one of the list has been made into a God, and a totally uncritical attitude adopted not only to all he is purported to have said and done, but also to the religious accretions which have accumulated in his name. Certainly I believe that the kind of proscription my friend ironically advocates would have the results he prophesies: but they would be a new expression, arising from the human situation as it then existed, not shaped, directed and seemingly sustained by images, forms and myths inherited from past institutions. They would be born of actual human need and conviction, and it is because religious dogma and ecclesiastical organization make these at least ambiguous if not totally irrelevant that my reaction against any kind of church doctrine had become so firm.

So we must now end this historical resume of a movement whose real history has not yet been lived, and consider at greater length my objections to Christian theology, so far as this has been traditionally propagated.

Section Three

NON-THEOLOGY

IN my article on non-church in *New Christian*, I had quoted from a letter I had received from a teen-aged girl in 1965 when I was editor of the magazine of the South London Industrial Mission, *Over the Bridge*. We had been conducting a correspondence on 'new' methods of worship, but this correspondent took the argument on to a different plain:

> No one can deny that the Church is doing a good thing in trying to 'reach' the young 'outside'. May I respectfully point out that it is failing miserably? This attempt to buy the young at the cost of their own dignity does not succeed. Nor would it, even if you had the Stones singing a Lennon-McCartney setting of the Magnificat. Why? Most of my friends do not go to church. This is because they cannot accept the existence of any form of spiritual Being. . . . Many older people too would, if honest with themselves, admit that the reason for their failure to attend church was a lack of belief in God. Atheism is not confined to a circle of highly intelligent doubters. It is for this reason that all teaching that presupposes a belief in God is valueless. It is no good preaching that Christ is the Son of God if people are going to say, 'What God?'[1]

The concept of God has been a convenient shorthand term in human parlance to epitomize a wide range of feelings, ideas, and experiences. I shall examine some of these, consider some of the contemporary approaches, and then state my own conclusions.

Amongst primitive man, *fear* was a basic motive for accepting and worshipping some deity. Life was short, brutal, cruel – a battle for survival in a context which presented many uncontrollable and incomprehensible elements. Existence itself depended on the elements – rain, warmth, fertility: if these failed, crops failed and men starved. It was natural in that situation that men should acknowledge, worship, and if necessary offer sacrifices to, the superior Being whom they conceived of as controlling these elements, and being able to withdraw them at will. In addition there was the multitude of natural factors in living which left men frightened because they could not understand them – earthquakes, volcanoes, thunder and lightning; even oddly-shaped trees or rocks, mountains, rivers and streams. Unusual people were viewed in the same way as having been 'touched' by their particular deity – the psychic, the mentally abnormal, the 'dedicated' or holy ones. It is not surprising that at these early stages of the evolutionary process, those who could capitalize on this fear – the priests, by whatever name they were termed – became all-powerful. Anyone who was considered capable of influencing the deity, or of inheriting some of his powers, was one to be treated with caution and obedience. Only at the time of the Renaissance – the last period when man made a new step forward in his evolution – was this authority broken; but it survives in primitive areas today, and in our western culture is exemplified in the obedience (so far as this is shown) of Roman Catholic families to the Pope's ruling on birth control.

This fear was allied to *ignorance*: and the term 'God' was given to those areas of life which man did not understand. This policy was subject to the law of diminishing returns, since the areas of lack of knowledge eventually fell to the inherent human quest for truth and understanding. Again, it is the post-Renaissance period which has viewed the most dramatic developments, pioneered by Newton, who, guided by Copernicus and Galileo, explained the solar system in natural terms (though even he, when queried about the earth's axis, explained it as caused by 'the hand of God' – a perfect example of the shorthand use of this term); and later periods saw the same process at work – Darwin 'removing' God from the sphere of creation, Freud from the subconscious, and so on. John Robinson has described this use of 'God' as the 'God of the gaps' approach; and it is this God which is no longer attractive or necessary to modern man.

The change in attitude here is particularly enlightening in three areas: disease, size of family, and outer space. In primitive societies disease was viewed as primarily a spiritual matter, and the man to deal with it was the priest or witch doctor. Today most people turn to the man with scientific training, who can offer the drugs most likely to cure their disease, or who has the surgical knowledge which will enable him to operate efficiently on their bodies.

Enduring much longer has been the concept that parents have the number of children that 'God sends them'. Today, parents increasingly make their own decision as to the size and spacing of their families. and although there remain the occasional 'mistakes' – when eagerness triumphs over wariness – modern methods of birth control are minimizing these; and with the advent of legalized abortions we are reaching the point where the only children to arrive in the world will be those who are desired and planned for.

The landing of men on the moon, and the implications of this for future space exploration, have changed the human attitude to the celestial spheres. William Hamilton[2] described how his young son gazed one night at the stars, but, unlike his ancestors with their overwhelming sense of awe, he asked tersely, 'Which one did we put up there, dad?' Some may regret that the technological age has the effect of reducing the element of wonder in the minds of many people; but this is healthy compared with the subservience to the natural spheres on the part of earlier generations. Perhaps one of the consequences of the technological revolution will be a rebirth of poetry as an important element in people's lives – the poet being the man who can bring to light as a cause for joy those areas and phenomena of living which his unenlightened contemporaries might otherwise view as purely functional.

Another use of the God-concept has been that of the *rectifier*. However one looks at life, whether optimistically or pessimistically, with cynicism or credulity, hope or despair, it is clear that people do not share the same opportunities, the same experiences of fulfilment, the same heights and depths of existence. For some, life is short, painful and deprived; for others filled with satisfaction and happiness. Some are in possession of all their faculties; others go through life handicapped physically or mentally; some have healthy lives, others are continually afflicted by disease; some live long, others die young – the variations are endless. How easy, therefore, to bring a degree of rationality into an otherwise totally irrational situation by introducing the concept of God, who 'will wipe all tears from our eyes' and compensate in the next life for what was lacking in this. It lent a degree of equity to an anomolous situation, and it is easy to see that for people in various ages, lands and degrees of distress it was an essential factor in remaining relatively sane. Its corollary was belief in a life after death, whether in some other world or again by reincarnation in this world, when the perseverance displayed in this existence would have its reward. It was this element of religion as preached in Victorian England which gave Marx his 'opium of the people' theme.

Today there is little need, in the western world at least, for this

God-image. Lives may be shallow, unfulfilled in terms of potential, and occasionally short: but for most people there is a reasonable standard of living, and the near certainty of experiencing enough years at least to feel that one has been around for a while. The pressure, in other words, is off; man has matters more in control; and so, short of a national disaster like war, or a personal bereavement, there is little psychological need to fall back on the rock that 'never lets man down' – simply because it remains a metaphysical image, untouchable by empirical enquiry. But as man continues to progress (and provided he doesn't take a wrong turning and annihilate himself and his fellows altogether) even this image will pale. For some this will be painful, but, in Plato's words, they will be dragged screaming from their caves to take upon themselves the responsibilities which their ancestors had so lightly (albeit understandably) handed over to 'God'. This God of the gaps cannot survive, if man is to inherit his birthright.

Is there then no area of life where God is not related to man at his weakest? Has not God stood in for man at his most learned, his most dedicated and his most compassionate levels? An answer to this was offered a century ago by Ludwig Feuerbach. His aim in *Das Wesen des Christentums* was to humanize theology, and much of it has a strangely contemporary ring. He argued that man is to himself his own object of thought. Religion is the consciousness of the infinite which man experiences in his deepest moments – the infinitude of knowledge, of the number and intensity of personal relationships, of creativity and work, and so on. To none of these can there ever be a limit; and this situation is tidied up by projecting the inner awareness of the infinity of personal consciousness to the image of a personal God, all-knowing, all-powerful, all-present, all-loving. So God is the outward projection of man's inward nature, and religion 'nothing else than the consciousness of the infinity of the consciousness; or, in the consciousness of the infinite, the conscious subject has for his object the infinity of his own nature'.[3]

Thus, God the great law-giver, God as love, God the all-wise, all correspond to some need in human nature. The danger, Feuerbach asserted, arose when man personalized this image to the extent of granting God a nature separate from his own. This resulted in what he termed a 'false and theological essence of religion' – 'religious materialism', with a belief in revelation and associated themes such as episcopacy, ordination, and the sacraments. Through these, man was, so to speak, hoist on his own petard, controlled by the image he himself had created. Men have consequently lived in fear at the thought of the Judgement Day, when this God would assess the worth of their brief lives, and determine whether they should 'enter into their joy' or join the worthless in some kind of 'outer darkness'. Others have spent their lives in self-immolation before this image, overwhelmed by a sense of their own worthlessness, weighed down with feelings of guilt. Even when men have acted lovingly, wisely, self-sacrificially, Christian theology, at least, has encouraged some kind of in-duced humility, whereby the agent attributes his worthwhileness to the 'grace' of God. The result is that, ironically, the image of God representing man-at-his-best has been just as deadly for man's achieving to the full the depth and riches of his own humanity as was that of man-at-his-weakest.

This explanation of the God image accounts for the particular form of self-deception with which many church people – and probably others as well – will be familiar: the claiming of divine authority for the opinion uttered. 'It is the will of God . . .' spoken before some recommended course of action means, at its best, 'I (we) consider that this is the best plan of procedure' and, at its worst, 'This particular policy suits my own interests best'. I remember informing an astonished audience in Bridgwater Town Hall at the time of the Suez fiasco, 'It is now the will of God that the Conservative government should resign'. Perhaps this public confession will help to expiate that piece of pious cant.

Let me at this point make one matter clear: I do not object to the use of 'God' as a shorthand term for the best values we know. On this basis the American educationist, Dewey, who would presumably be described by the orthodox as an atheist, could write of God as a 'unification of ideal values', ideals acknow-ledged 'at a given time and place' as authoritative, and also as 'connected with all the natural forces and conditions . . . that promote the growth of the ideal'.[4] It explains why 'God' has given men strength and courage, since a coordination of awareness of what is good, and right, and true can clearly give a unity and consistency of purpose lacking in many men without this image. By the same token, however, if the image is of something less than the ideal, tarnished by greed and hatred and lust, evil deeds can be, and have often been, performed in God's name. God is only truly God when men, or an individual man, can represent the best, whether in terms of intellect, action, or emotions.

It was something along these lines that Tillich was trying to present with his teaching of God as 'the ground of our being', and which John Robinson was expressing in *Honest to God*. Yet Robinson states that we are put on 'very dangerous ground' by Bultmann's answer to a challenge from Karl Barth: 'I would heartily agree: I *am* trying to substitute anthropology for theology for I am interpreting theological affirmations as assertions about human life.' He proceeds to criticize Feuerbach:

> For, to Feuerbach, to say that 'theology is nothing else than anthropology' means that 'the knowledge of God is nothing else than a knowledge of man'. And his system runs into the deification of man, taken to its logical conclusion in the Superman of Nietzsche and Auguste Comte's Religion of Humanity.
> . . . The question inevitably arises, if theology is translated into anthropology, why do we any longer need the category of God? Is it not 'semantically superfluous'?[5]

My own view is that the term is almost entirely 'semantically superfluous' though, as we have seen, it is often used as a shorthand expression for qualities which are difficult to express, and certainly cannot be expressed briefly; but it *is* a barrier to communication for the reason I have indicated: it lays itself open to a wide variety of interpretations. It is possible for one man to state 'I believe in God' (meaning a term summarizing ideal human values, but rejecting any kind of personalization); and for another to state 'I don't believe in God' (meaning a personalized being), so that, despite the apparent total contradiction in the two statements, both express roughly the same beliefs. It is absurd that such a possibility should exist, and in any other sphere of life clarification would, rightly, be demanded. If, for instance, one man's interpretation of love was compassion, while another's was simply desire for possession, how could they without further clarification discuss what 'loving one's neighbour' mean. (This is in fact a bad example, since this English word is open to a wide range of interpretations in any case: but it makes its point in that the confusion which sometimes arises when considering what love in practice means indicates the need for precision when using it. It allows for the old German joke:

> *Der schlimmste Feind, merk' dir es wohl,*
> *Er ist der böse Alkohol:*
> *Doch in der Bibel steht geschrieben:*
> '*Du musst auch deine Feinde lieben.*')

John Robinson says of his book: 'The beginning is to try to be honest – and to go on from there.' I suggest that one step further along the way is to drop altogether the word 'God' unless we are committed to an acceptance of the personal being 'in whom we live, and move, and have our being,' from whom we come, and to whom we go. It seems hardly necessary to point out that if we continue to maintain this fiction, we remain in the dubious situation of having to explain how, in a world created by an omnipotent being, who is allegedly at the same time all-loving, so many thousands of millions of lives are stunted by malnutrition, disease, and illiteracy. We may understand and applaud the dedication of many who believe in him, and as a consequence of this belief work self-sacrificially to alleviate the evils of the world; but we shall be no nearer understanding why the diseases and other evils exist in the first place. To attribute them to man is an affront to human intelligence: how did *man* create leprosy? To see them as a challenge to man is an evasion: so was Hitler's menace in Europe.

The only escape route is the creation of yet another myth, epitomized in the self-sacrifice of Jesus: the God who shares the suffering of his own world. This is at least more satisfactory than the legend of the purifying and sanctifying effect of suffering; it is more intellectually satisfying than the concept of suffering as vicarious – as if the two-thirds of the world who starve are somehow benefiting spiritually the non-starving third, or the two-thirds of South Africa which is black the one third that is white. But it still leaves unanswered the problem of *why* suffering on such a massive scale exists. Once the concept of a personal, loving God is laid to rest, the problem of suffering can be viewed for what it is: a consequence of living at all in a world full of a variety of menaces, conditioned by chance, and with no inbuilt purpose to fulfil except in terms of the solar system as a whole. Within this situation man is called on to meet the problems exemplified in human suffering, and to overcome them. (And if it be argued that God is at work in the doctors and teachers and Gospel workers engaged in this, one can only say that the abhorrence of anti-vivisectionists to experiments on animals cannot be compared with the loathing one must feel towards a being who uses human lives in order to encourage skill and dedication.)

How far have the 'death of God' theologians served the anti-theistic (as opposed to atheistic) approach which I am advocating? I doubt if they have helped the cause of replacing theology with anthropology by the use of this phrase. God is hardly a term of whom death can be predicated. If by God is meant a spiritual entity, then by definition death is impossible; if a symbol of human infinitude, then its continued use disproves the assertion. However, those involved in the movement have contributed considerably to the wider cause of de-theologizing human values. Nietzsche's original use of the phrase will help to clarify why this is so. He tells of the madman who cried out in the market-place:

> Where is God gone? I mean to tell you! We have killed Him – you and I! We are all His murderers! . . . God is dead! God remains dead! And we have killed Him! . . . Is not the magnitude of this deed too great for us? Shall we not ourselves have to become Gods, merely to seem worthy of it? There never was a greater event – and on account of it, all who are born after us belong to a higher history than any history hitherto!

Thus the phrase summarizes the desire that men shall accept responsibility for their own, and their neighbours', destinies. In practice, according to William Hamilton, this means that whatever underlay the concept of God must be replaced partly by Jesus, partly by the community. Of the latter he writes:

> We must learn to forgive each other with the radical un-conditioned grace men used to ascribe to God. We must learn to comfort each other, and we must learn to judge, check and rebuke each other in the communities within which we are wounded, and in which we are healed. If these things cannot now be done by the human communities in the world, then these communities must be altered until they can perform these tasks and whatever others, once ascribed to God, that need to be done in this new context. In this sense the death of God leads to politics, to social change, and even to the foolishness of utopias.[6]

This thought corresponds with John Robinson's suggestion that man is no longer seeking a gracious God, but a gracious neighbour.

That man cannot exist on his own is manifest. But in place of the grace of God, the supernatural assistance allegedly bestowed on man with a view to his sanctification, must come the assistance of others in the community, who are in turn strengthened and encouraged by himself. This may be written off as the bee-hive complex suggested by one of my correspondents, but this is damning by use of an unflattering analogy. If we replaced this with the analogy of heaven, and state simply that all the conditions of unity and love predicated of this must be found in human communities on earth, it will be seen that the task is infinitely wide, the opportunities for depth of relationship infinitely extensive and satisfying.

It is akin to Buber's advocacy of the I-Thou relationship, in which a description of the 'I' involves the 'Thou' since each is affected by and dependent on the other. Both speak and act in relation, rather than in the detachment which typifies 'I – it' relationships. Thus those deeply involved relationships described as 'I – thou' replace God; or rather, God is seen as the 'thou' of a man's life, those people, and hopes, and aspirations, and involvements which are the pivot to all he undertakes.

Hamilton suggests that 'death of God' theology follows in a natural line of succession from the writings of such people as Blake, Hegel, Strauss, Feuerbach, Marx, Ibsen, Strindberg, George Eliot, Matthew Arnold, Hawthorne and Melville; and he sees the present age as remarkable in that so-called Christian theologians and so-called atheists – such as Camus and Pasternak – are to be found arguing from virtually the same premises. Both groups would not, for instance, reckon the classical statement of Augustine's to be valid in their lives: 'Thou hast made us for thyself, and our hearts can find no rest until they are at rest in thee.' Hamilton sees the end-product of this situation one in which the idea of God lives on, but without any conception of his sphere of work. This is already happening, and explains why the one area of life which remains a mystery – death – is the one in which people are most likely to introduce the name of God into the conversation. For most of his life, western man today is untheistic, if not atheistic. Feuerbach had affirmed that these were themselves increasingly meaningless terms. The real difference in people sprang not from whether or not they affirmed a belief in a personal deity, but whether they acknowledged that such attributes as truth, love, and so on were of value. The real 'athcists' today are those who acknowledge no values to living, whose standards are based on solely materialistic appraisals of what is of worth, and who in consequence are incapable of any kind of relationship worthy of that name.

I have already quoted Hamilton to show that such 'great' New Testament words as grace are not 'lost' but simply redirected if we follow the approach proposed throughout this section. Here is how one of the non-church correspondents suggested rewriting the first commandment of Jesus:

Remember at all times that life, whether of the individual or of the human race, is not something earned or acquired on merit, which it is for us to dispose of as we will, but a free gift which the individual and the race alike misuse at their peril and have it in their power ultimately to destroy.

Some may see this transference of thought from the theological to the anthropological as a reduction, but insofar as it meets the real need of modern man – within the life he knows, and amid the situations with which he is confronted – it must be viewed as an enhancement.

Revelation and the 'Supernatural'

Any attempt to transfer theological concepts to the sphere of anthropology must come to terms with the fact and experience of revelation, accepting Aquinas's classical distinction between truths of reason and truths of revelation, whether these be viewed as differences in kind or only in degree. Is it not a continual experience of the human species that many of their thoughts, feelings, actions are induced or motivated not from within themselves but from agencies, or an agency, without? Can we contemplate man throughout history without seeing him as, at least in part and possibly primarily, one who *re*acts, *res*ponds, rather than proceeding on his own initiative? What shall be said about the experience of the mystics, the beatific vision? How does one explain such experiences as the conversion of St Paul, or St Augustine, or Wesley's heart being 'strangely warmed'?

There seems no reason either, on the one hand, to belittle revelation, in whatever form it be manifested, or, on the other, to posit a separate divine entity, God, consciously 'calling' or in some manner influencing those whom he has chosen. Revelation in its various manifestations must be interpreted as an individual's reaction to the various external influences around him. These may be caused by certain elements in the community in which he is placed; by expressions of creativity, such as art or music; by the natural surroundings; by the mysteries of birth and of death; by the fusion through sex of two personalities into one, as a man and a woman soar 'beyond our bourne of time and place'; by the response of those whose work makes great demands upon them, so that they feel themselves challenged, tested, 'stretched'; by moments of tranquillity, such as people may feel when sitting in a great cathedral, or in a communion service; and in those moments when words spoken or written suddenly bring a new 'truth' to light in the listener's or reader's mind, so that the subjective experience is that of illumination from without rather than any kind of self-originating comprehension.

Of course, *how* these experiences affect us as they do remains to a great extent unknown. But perhaps as increasingly we learn to 'know ourselves' – as young children are encouraged to ask themselves why they experience a sense of awe, wonder, or mystery in certain situations – we shall be better equipped to explain this; and perhaps then these experiences, most of which happen unexpectedly, rarely, and refuse to lend themselves to being automatically induced, will be accepted as a natural part of man's birthright which can be continually experienced throughout life, so that the added dimension they provide will be viewed as normal.

To the extent, therefore, that we are looking for a natural rather than a supernatural interpretation of these and other phenomena, the human species as a whole is likely to benefit, since, by definition, a supernatural interpretation leaves the experiences beyond human control or enquiry. This conclusion seems reasonable even in the face of the experience of the mystics. Here is a how Ronald Hepburn, a humanist, has written of these experiences:

> There are certain types of religious experience, senses as of the 'holy', some forms also of mystical experience that, for some people at least, can continue to occur even in agnosticism. They seem in this sense to be 'autonomous', not belief-dependent, experiences. Even if they are not seen as yielding new knowledge of the world, insights into 'ultimate truth', they can still make a profound mark on a person's moral outlook. They can do so, not by imparting specific new information or specific rules of conduct but by nourishing a sense of wondering openness to new ways, new possibilities of life. They implant a disturbing restlessness, a *nisus* towards the transformation of ideals, an intensified dissatisfaction with the mean, drab or trivial. . . . Mystical experience, in many if not all of its forms, is experience of reconciliation, the breaking down of barriers of individuality. It can be brought into intimate relation with movements of thought and feeling in morality, such as sympathetic identification with others, escape from egocentricity to the stance of charity. Nature-mystical experiences, even in quite lowly and undeveloped forms, can foster and reinforce

> attitudes of contemplative gentleness and restraint in our
> dealings with nature, and can act as a powerful corrective to
> the dominant attitudes of technological man.'[7]

Thus, in turning from theology to anthropology, no attempt is being made to ignore or belittle those experiences which give life its 'tang'. It is the interpretation which is rejected – as we rejected the idea of ordination as the divine 'stamp' on a man – not their reality. If some prefer to describe their experiences in terms of the supernatural, they are entitled to do so; but they should not criticize, because they need not feel challenged by, those who are not so inclined. For many people, neither the depth nor the reality of these 'extra-normal' experiences are enhanced by positing the concept of God as the originator of the revelation concerned, however ethereal this may seem to be when contemplated by man the recipient. Since the whole of life is a process of action, inter-action, and reaction, it would be surprising if the element summarized as revelation were not manifestly present.

The concept of *life after death* must similarly be accounted for in terms of the human condition, human need, human motivation. As already outlined in reference to the concept of God, the lack of equity in life has predicated for many people a further life in which justice may be seen to be done. Having accepted the prior concept of a loving, all-seeing God, the consequent need for an afterlife became doubly necessary. In addition, when life was short and brutal, and there were few moments of 'glory' contained in it, and nothing to look forward to except decay and death, it is hardly surprising that sights were set on the 'happy land, far, far away' or to the heaven where 'all God's children got shoes'. For many men and women caught up in the inhumanity of the industrial revolution two centuries ago, this vision must have been a light to keep them sane. For many, especially in backward countries, it no doubt remains so today. But clearly, as man progresses and more people everywhere become reasonably assured of a normal life-span, ending with a natural decline in physical and mental faculties, death will be seen as the final process of living, not far removed from the stage immediately preceding it.

I cannot understand why anyone should wish to posit a theory of survival regarding those who die in old age, whose faculties have waned to the point of non-existence. They then cease to exist, except as an individual memory in the minds and lives of their surviving family and friends. I can understand why the

94

human frame is profoundly disturbed by premature death – in war, in an accident, through an illness. In these circumstances, plans, processes, courses of living, unexpectedly cease to be, and all security is momentarily shattered – lasting for some people for the remainder of their lives. Yet it does not seem to me to be one whit more humble, or holy, or profound to view such accidents as part of some wider providential plan for the world. At the actual moment of close personal bereavement it may be therapeutic to accept a fatalistic outlook, but this would be an unhealthy approach to life as a whole. Whether, for example, deaths on the roads will be reduced or not depends entirely on human care, skill, and planning. Disease can be overcome only through the research and knowledge of man. The destructiveness of war will cease only when man learns to accept and live with all his fellows – and takes infinitely greater care in determining the numbers inhabiting this planet. Inasmuch as none of these problems have yet been solved, and their total removal from life will be only a gradual process anyway, there will still be those who lose out – those who are destroyed in an accident, or by a disease, or an act of aggression, beyond their own personal control. This must be viewed as one of the risks of living. To exist at all is to live dangerously. Having accepted the risk from the start, or having come to terms with it at some stage of life, it is possible to proceed with a fair degree of equanimity. To add the extra dimension of life after death seems to me to be refusing to come to terms with life.

Obviously, among those who accept an afterlife as their personal destiny, a distinction must be made between those who yet feel that their main task in this world is to proceed with living, and to be immersed in the activities and relationships which this provides, and those whose sights are permanently fixed on the next life. For the former, the idea of survival is a reassuring concept at the back of their minds. (Perhaps this is nature's way of compensating man for his very awareness that he is going to die.) For these people, so far as progress towards making a 'heaven of earth' is concerned, belief in a life after death is hardly a disruptive factor.

However, it is less possible to view with equanimity those in the second category. As Camus wrote:

> If there is a sin against life, it is not perhaps so much to despair of life, as to hope for another life and to lose sight of the implacable grandeur of this one.[8]

It may be argued against this that the so-called 'implacable grandeur' is not always immediately obvious in life, and that some people never discover this. Pictures of this world as a 'vale of tears', of its 'brief sorrow, short-lived care', of men and women 'toil-worn and sad', of the 'mortal affliction' of life abound in Christian hymnology, liturgy, and devotional writings. As a description of some people's lives they are no doubt accurate enough; as a general description of life they are offensive. One wonders if those who claim not to have found the 'implacable grandeur' would still affirm this if they knew they were shortly to be executed. Would not a love for the 'pure flame of life' which is in them be predominant in their minds?

It seems, therefore, that man will gradually reach stages of development in which increasingly those elements in life which threaten it most will be overcome: and concomitantly the psychological need for belief in a life after death will lessen, if not entirely disappear. This will not remove a sense of dissatisfaction from the minds of those who look for a logical progression in living. It will not remove the irony that though man may expect to become wiser as he grows older, he will yet cease in a moment to exist, and his wisdom generally die with him. But to object to this is like a man who has won £5000 objecting that it was not £10,000. His reflection should be that at least he has lived, shared in the joys and potentialities of existence, been enriched by the presence of others, helped to enrich their lives: and at the last he will simply go the way of all flesh, like every other living creature. To misquote Tennyson: ''Tis better to have lived and died Than never to have lived at all.'

I cannot believe that this outlook can be anything but salutary. It concentrates human faculties on the present, on the human situation as it exists, and must be a goad towards improving the lot of mankind generally. It will not necessarily rid the world of martyrs (assuming that these will be required in the future) but will make more poignant any sacrificial death on the part of men or women who prefer non-existence to the type of existence forced upon them. Indeed, if the prospect is to sleep with no chance to dream the choice before a man facing that which he would rather die than do becomes more straightforward.

But this would be a morbid note on which to end this particular discussion. The situation we can contemplate is one in which fulfilment in a wider number of areas of life will become possible

for an increasingly widening range of people. It is to this fulfilment, here and now, both personally and socially, that we should
be directing ourselves. Life may be brief, but it need not be
shallow: the implications of this I leave till the final section.

Forgiveness

What then of divine forgiveness? Does this too have no further
relevance in human life, despite the fact that many, both in the
past and today, have felt the need of it, have experienced it, and
have expressed this experience in 'supernatural' terms?

There are two things to be said about this. The first was mentioned when considering the death of God theology, and quoting
from William Hamilton (page 90). It is part of the responsibility
of the *community* to offer the sense of forgiveness to its members.
In other words, the community must be an accepting community,
giving the support to each individual as he requires it. There can
be no ostracizing, no barriers between an individual and the rest:
where such barriers exist, a community composed of mature
individuals will overcome them. This may seem to be stating an
impossible ideal, but it is really only a wider extension of the
family spirit, expressed to varying degrees in factories, firms,
colleges and schools. To be accepted – not to feel that one's
past or present cuts one off from those in the environment: this
is a deeply-felt need, as is evinced, for instance, in the continuing popularity of the 'Coronation Street' series, about a
community where something of this forgiving process takes
place. It should – to bring the matter down to grass-roots prac-
ticality – be one of the major factors influencing town planners:
too many environments are built without any consideration for
potential human contacts. (That this can be done is shown in
the Hyde Park experiment in Sheffield.) The top priority for
today's planners must be to ensure that the environment creates
opportunities for communal therapy.

The second point is probably even more important. The first
requisite, where forgiveness is required, is forgiveness of self.
Even for a person who continues to believe in God, this is still
true, if the harm caused by a sense of guilt is to be obviated.
Many a person has been assured, either through the private
words of a priest or through the Absolution in public worship,
that his sins are forgiven; but if he yet remains guilt-ridden he
will stay unhappy, morbid, neurotic or even suicidal. Until he has
forgiven himself for what he has done, no words of a priest, and
no concept of divine forgiveness, will penetrate deeply into his

personality so as to affect his later thoughts and actions. It is a logical step from this to suggest that while for some – either from force of habit or from profound conviction – the assurance of divine forgiveness remains of value, for the majority this is no longer so, provided they are mature enough to forgive themselves. This thought is expressed in Hemingway's *For Whom the Bell Tolls*. Anselmo is speaking to Jordan about his hopes for life after the war:

'But if I live later, I will try to live in such a way, doing no harm to anyone, that it will be forgiven.'

'By whom?'

'Who knows? Since we do not have God here any more, neither His Son nor the Holy Ghost, who forgives? I do not know.'

'You have not God any more?'

'No. Man. Certainly not. If there were God, never would He have permitted what I have seen with my eyes. Let *them* have God.'

'They claim Him.'

'Clearly I miss Him, having been brought up in religion. But now a man must be responsible to himself.'

'Then it is thyself who will forgive thee for killing.'

'I believe so,' Anselmo said.

What is being suggested here, and what I believe the general viewpoint of this section inevitably leads to, is that if a man feels himself to be alienated from other people, he is therefore also alienated from himself; so any attempt to overcome this alienation will depend in the first place upon himself. Only when he has accepted, or come to terms with, himself, will he be able to sense that he is also accepted by other people; and once he has experienced *this* acceptance, he is able (or enabled) to give himself positively to and for his fellows. He will then be on his way to discovering what modern psychologists tend to call 'life in depth', what Jesus called 'abundant life', and what the disciples called 'resurrection'. The fact that the myths on which traditional expressions of this experience were founded have been discarded does not mean that the experience is any less real, or any less obtainable. It was the 'atheist' Camus who wrote: 'In the middle of winter, I at last discovered that there was in me an invincible summer.'

What can we say today with certainty about Jesus? And when we have decided the answer to that question, is there any need to say it? These are the two questions to which I wish to apply myself at this point; and it will be possible only to suggest various points and pass on, though I recognize that each of them has ramifications which could engage the energies of a score of writers.

It is essential from the start, with Bultmann and his successors, to make a clear distinction between the historical Jesus and the mythical Christ. In other words, we must distinguish between the man-as-he-was and the image of him held by successive individuals and societies. This is unfortunately not taking one's understanding very far forward, since there remains the problem of delineating in the Gospels between what Jesus actually did and said, and what others stated he did and said. The myth overlaps the history. From Paul, through the Gospels, with their different accounts of the way Jesus was preached about in various early Christian communities, we have a series of interpretations of his life and message, almost certainly none of which were written by actual eye-witnesses of his ministry. Paul gives us few references to the life or words of Jesus, but provides the basis for a *summa theologica*; God self-emptied in Christ, Jesus, the risen victorious Lord, and so on. Mark provides a more down-to-earth picture, with little emphasis on the teaching of Jesus, but much on the contacts and conflicts he encountered throughout his ministry. Matthew gives us more the picture of Jesus the Rabbi; Luke the more humane picture of the friend of sinners and outcasts. John provides a portrait based on the theology of the incarnate word; the letter to the Hebrews that of the great high priest; Revelation that of the Lamb of God, the eternal Victim.

Obviously this is a potted summary which demands infinitely more detailed analysis; but the point stands: the New Testament is a series of images, sometimes with a theological superstructure added, of the man Jesus, reflecting either the point of view of the writer, or the picture held by a particular community towards the end of the first century of our era, and on through the second.

This has been the process throughout history: different ages have had their different images of Christ, and in any one age different people have possessed theirs. Thus Jesus has been proclaimed the sacramental Christ, the Judge of the world, the Saviour, the inaugurator of a new era, the Head of his body, the

Church, and, in our own age 'the man for others'. Alongside these have been secondary interpretations, such as the image of the meek Christ, the romantic Christ, Christ the socialist/pacifist/communist/revolutionary. The latest expression to reach me chooses six images: teacher, healer, compassion, law of love, righteousness and mankind offered to God.[9] In other words, 'Christ' has symbolized whatever in any particular age or place men of insight felt that they and their fellows most needed to meet their mental, spiritual or physical wants. In time of death Christ is the one who has conquered death; in sickness the one who co-ordinates man's faculties and so brings wholeness; in temptation the one who overcame temptation and won through; in trial the one who suffered and endured to the end; in human communication the one who could break down barriers; in sorrow the one who was acquainted with grief. The list is almost endless.

The phrase which has become the most firmly entrenched in Christian theology is Son of God, and this is the key to the others. If we interpret God along the lines suggested earlier, we are implying by this phrase that the image we have of Jesus is of one who responded at every point in his life to the ground of his being – to the best that was in him, to the 'thou' of his life. In him, in other words, we have an image of life at its best, when all the secondary, ulterior elements are relegated to almost, if not total, non-existence. All man's aspirations, his sense of the infinitude of knowledge, of depth of relationship, of areas of fulfilment, are epitomized in the image of one who achieved as many of these as the human frame and a short life can achieve. Naturally, certain elements were closely related to convictions of the age in which the image was first given utterance: thus it was inevitable that the image should not be of a married Christ, or of a scholar or intellectual.

So, when Christian devotion is directed towards 'Christ', it means that people are turning back for strength, guidance and encouragement to that image which has enabled their forefathers to discover or rediscover these qualities. They are reminding themselves of the ideal; and since it is difficult to carry this in mind as a series of statements or rules, the continuing expression of this image of the ideal human being through successive generations is something to be both understood and admired. So powerful and universal has it been, that even many who would have nothing to do with theological statements – like Mahatma Gandhi – have accepted it as the most therapeutic of all in the human situation. William Hamilton, speaking about the 'death of God' shows how this image replaces the concept of God held in earlier ages:

> If by God you mean the focus of obedience, the object of trust and loyalty, the meaning I give to love, my center, my meaning – then these meanings are given not to men in general but to Jesus, the *man*, in his life, his way with others, and his death. . . . We see as the center of the Christian faith a relation of obedience and trust directed to Jesus.[10]

Is there, then, a historical person behind the myth, the image? The evidence for this has usually been presented in terms of the effect of the image on the subsequent development of human society, especially in the civilization of the west, rather than in concrete empirical terms. It is suggested that history would hardly have been split in two over a myth, and that the name Jesus would not have become the most revered name in history if there had been no such person. I doubt if this kind of evidence proves any more than the power of an idea when it touches mankind at the deepest level. Judaism dates the years according to a myth, and insofar as the concept of Christ has been the most dynamic, so far, in the history of man there seems nothing incongruous or improbable about dating the years from the time of the alleged birth of the mythical figure.

All I am trying to imply by making this point is that it would in no way make a mockery of the western world's dating of the years if it could be proved that no such person as Jesus had ever lived. The Christ-myth would be just as real, just as powerful in many people's lives, if it could be shown that the account of Jesus's life and teaching were the end-product of a process which had been developed over a period of centuries among the people who are generally accredited to have been religious geniuses; and that this account epitomizes in the story of one man's life their latest and most profound insights about the human situation. It would help us to understand more the great differences between various elements in the teaching of Jesus. Stevie Smith, for instance, has written:

> And the penal sentences of Christ: He that believeth
> And is baptized shall be saved, he that believeth not
> Shall be damned. Depart from me ye cursed into everlasting
>   fire
> Prepared for the devil and his angels. And then,
> Saddest of all the words in scripture, the words,
> They went into everlasting punishment. Is this good?[11]

Instead of having to explain these words away as a Jewish-flavoured interpolation, or as an indication of a type of community within which such words would find acceptance, we should simply say that, like the reference to the iota of the law which would not pass away, they reflect one of the elements in the teaching about the Son of God which was peripheral to the central insights of the Gospels, and were eventually to be rejected generally as being alien to the central image. (It should be added, however, that this penal imagery has found acceptance among some propounders of the Christ-myth, not least those who follow the school of theology exemplified in Billy Graham.)

It would appear to me to be going too far, however, to state that there was no historical person, Jesus of Nazareth. Since he left no book, and lived in an age before a television company could record a 'Face to Face' with him for posterity, we are left with a mixture of myth and history which it will not be possible completely to unravel. But from the number of brief descriptive episodes certain traits emerge which seem to bear the stamp of flesh and blood. Paul Van Buren has expressed it in this way:

> The history available to us from the existing documents would not enable us to trace the course of Jesus's career, either externally or internally, but there is a great deal of material which gives us his history in the form of incidents. The task, then, is not to try to write a biography, but to catch the glimpses of the man, Jesus of Nazareth. They can be seized from the many little episodes which make up the Gospel tradition. In each of them, the figure at the centre stands out boldly, even if we are unable to say just when and where the occurrence took place. From all these fragments, and from the way in which the early church responded to him, the originality and distinctiveness of the figure of Jesus of Nazareth may be seen.[12]

(It may be added that Reginald Fuller has indicated how a new quest of the historical Jesus is taking place, and I refer the reader to his book for a precise but wide-embracing survey of trends in New Testament scholarship.[13])

What then emerges from the narratives? To decide which elements reflect the myth of Christ rather than the historicity of Jesus is an impossible task, and conclusions will vary according to the person who makes the assessment. The point to affirm strongly is that any picture will be subjective: have any two 'lives' of Jesus been the same? All one can be sure of is that certain narratives certainly belong to the myth – such as the nature miracles, the raisings from the dead, most of John's Gospel, references to the Son of God. This is not in any way to belittle the importance of these: whether historical or mythical, they are important if they influence people's lives. Equally, whether historical or mythical, they are unimportant if they do not. There can be no objective truth, either in the life of Jesus or in the myth of Christ. Both of these are 'true' only to the extent that people are changed by them.

The three elements in the Gospel narratives which seem to be paramount in the delineation of Jesus are the man of compassion, the man of authority, and the man of freedom. I think the last of these is the key to them all, and explains why the myth of Christ the Messiah, which had been prominent in Jewish piety and teaching for some centuries, should focus itself eventually on him. He was free *from racial and national barriers* – man-created conceptions of fundamental differences between people which to Jesus apparently did not exist. He was free *from any subservience to the Jewish authorities*, and seems to have spent much of his ministry engaged in clashes of one kind or another with them.[14] Above all, he was free *from the Jewish law*, free in his approach to take it or leave it according to its furtherance or otherwise of human needs and values. So, we find Jesus reacting favourably not only to the Jews, with whom he naturally spent most of his time, but also to the Samaritans whom the Jews despised, the Greeks whom they hated, the Romans whom they feared. Then he speaks his woes over the scribes and Pharisees – abrasive words which are, not surprisingly but perhaps unfortunately, seldom read out in churches; and finally he rejected most if not all of the Sabbath regulations imposed on the people, and even discarded the Old Testament where he felt its teaching to be inadequate when faced with the human predicament: 'You have heard that it was said of old . . . but I say unto you . . .'

The freedom of Jesus was freedom for, as well as freedom from. Being freed from the normal debilitating considerations which impose weighty restrictions on the lives of most people – the desire for popularity (especially among the 'people who count'), concern for status, desire to be recognized and acknowledged – Jesus was free for others. He was at their disposal. (The French have the ideal word for this quality: disponibilité, which is only half-translated by the English word availability. It is a key word in the Taizé Community.) It is this freedom which made possible both the depth and the extent of Jesus's compassion. While this had limits – like any other human being Jesus had periods when he had to get away from people – there is the sense that he was open to the cares and needs and hopes and fears of all those whom he encountered. That this did not produce merely a soft-hearted sentimentality is indicated by the incident of the money-changers, besides the clashes with the Pharisees already mentioned. His compassion was based on a real understanding of what motivated people.

The death of Jesus seems also, paradoxically enough, to be related to this freedom. I admit that at this point I may well be reading into the narrative my own interpretation of the myth. Schweitzer may have been right in asserting that Jesus went to his death in the mistaken belief that the long-prophesied Messianic Kingdom would thereby be inaugurated: on that interpretation his death was an error of judgement. Equally, however, one could state that where a man puts himself in the hands of others, he is at the mercy of the most selfish, as well as the weakest, or the noblest, in human nature. It epitomizes the great mystery – perhaps the single central truth which Christianity has given to the world – that love and sacrifice are two sides of the same coin; that, in fact, to love at all in this world is to live dangerously.

This freedom also, I think, explains Jesus's authority. This was not the authority of physical strength, such as we see in any autocratic state; it was not the authority of the expert, the specialist in some area of study – Jesus was no intellectual. It was not the authority which is delegated, so that small men wield a power and influence out of all proportion to their natural significance as people. It was hardly, in the strictest sense, a moral authority, though in the clashes with the religious rulers this is perhaps the best explanation. In general, Jesus's authority was one of personality. He seems to have been one of those rare men who possess an inward assurance, not demonstrated by any overbearing or insufferable self assertion, but by a quiet confidence which affects any who come into their presence. It is the authority of the man who never acts or speaks hastily, simply because he understands human beings and the human situation better than others, and therefore has any situation well in hand. It was an authority which impressed even the Roman Procurator, Pilate.

All these elements together seem to me to be the natural explanation of why the Christ myth eventually rested on this man. He was a charismatic person who could stimulate, foment, and profoundly disturb people to an extent rarely seen elsewhere in history, and perhaps uniquely. If different communities, generations, and individuals have been carried along by the effect of his personality to the extent of reading into it all their most exalted aspirations and profoundest yearnings about human nature in general, and their own in particular, this is a 'consummation devoutly to be desired'. It explains why Christian devotional writings abound with the writers' sense of actually communicating with him, and why this sense has been shared by many Christians over the centuries. 'I heard the voice of Jesus say . . .' and similar expressions brought into comprehensible perspective the best that was in them.

How then is the Resurrection to be interpreted? Its central role in Christian teaching prevents us on the one hand from ignoring it and on the other from reducing it to a fairy story of a corpse literally coming back to life. The meaning of the Resurrection does not depend either on a body evaporating through its grave-clothes, or on an empty tomb. To take the literalistic view not only reduces the episode to a tale of 'magic long ago': it also involves a misconception of the nature of a symbol. The trouble is that, while the New Testament narratives were written by Semites with non-literal minds, they have been interpreted largely by westerners with a prosaic mentality. To the Semite, the question of whether an incident were 'true' or not was, where symbolism was involved, a non-question. When Jeremiah wore his yoke to symbolize the affliction of Israel, the answer of his enemies was not to debate with him and point out that a wooden yoke was not a nation's agony: they broke the yoke. Thus the yoke was, and was not, that which it symbolized. So similarly with the Resurrection: to ask whether this actually happened is to ask the wrong question. What matters is what the Resurrection means; and it is to this that the New Testament writings apply themselves.

The earliest narrative simply states that 'he was raised on the third day . . . and appeared to Cephas, then to the twelve. . . Then he appeared to James, then to all the apostles. Last of all, as to one untimely born, he appeared also to me.'[15] Thus Paul makes no distinction between these 'appearances'; he puts his own experience on the Damascus road in the same category as the apostles'.

The operative word in this account is 'appeared'. Van Buren notes[16] that it is passive, not active; it does not state that the apostles *saw* Jesus; it is a statement of 'sense-content' which expresses an image 'on the mirror of the mind'. They had known Jesus in one sense, and at their lowest moment they had failed this Jesus; but now they saw him in a totally new way, a way so unexpected that it filled them with rapture; they saw him 'in a new light'. This new light changed them from the dejected group of failures that they had been to a group of men and women who realized that the authority, the freedom, the love of Jesus were 'contagious' (Van Buren's word) in the sense that a group of people can 'catch' the mood of a member of the group; and where this is the strongest personality in the group, the effect he has is so much the greater. Jesus, they saw, had become the great liberator, and all men could consequently share the fruit of this, whether in freedom from fear, from the 'sin' which restricted their lives and marred their relationships, or from religion in the traditional sense of established supernatural power (summed up by Paul as 'principalities and powers').

This interpretation is strengthened rather than invalidated by Paul's words, later in the same chapter, 'If Christ be not risen, then is your faith vain.' Christ is the symbol of that which was given flesh and blood in Jesus; and if, just because Jesus died an ignominious death, it be therefore assumed that all that he stood for throughout his life were invalidated, there could be no faith, among his followers and their successors, in the values which he exemplified. But once it was recognized that these values were untouchable by suffering, or punishment, or death, yet could, and would, take root in men's lives, thence to influence their decisions, their personalities, their relationships, their characters, then Christ, in whom were summed up all these values, had indeed risen from the dead: and many people since the first century have borne eloquent testimony to the truth of this by the lives they have lived.

Although there appears to be a conflict between this interpretation and that of the four Gospels, this is more apparent than real. Mark's Gospel, assuming chapter 16 verse eight to be the original ending, ends with the promise that Jesus is 'going before' the disciples to Galilee; Matthew's is fuller but contains obvious mythical embellishments – the earthquake, the angel of the Lord sitting on the stone – and has its climax in the promise 'Lo I am with you always'. Luke's narrative adds two further accounts: the appearance on the Emmaus road, with the words which give the key to it: 'Was it not necessary that the Christ should suffer these things and enter into his glory?' – a pregnant piece of symbolic writing. Then comes the difficult story of Jesus's eating some fish, followed by his injunction 'that repentance and forgiveness of sins should be preached in his name to all nations', and the promise of 'power from on high' – a promise which was to be fulfilled in the disciples and others, once they understood that the qualities personified in Jesus were in fact 'contagious'. John's Gospel links this receiving of power with the appearance of Jesus (20, 22) and leads to the original vivid climax: 'Blessed are those who have not seen, and yet have believed.' Chapter 21 seems to have been motivated by problems relating to the positions in the Christian community, and in Christian teaching generally, of Peter and John.

To construct a rigid dogma of actual physical rising from the dead from these narratives seems therefore unwarranted, on the grounds of the paucity of the evidence, the conflict of facts (where such an important event was concerned), and the obvious symbolic nature of the stories. We are, as I understand it, at a rare point in history: the birth of a myth which was to be life-enhancing for a wide range of people throughout successive centuries. The powerful impact of 'Christ' for two thousand years has justified the myth, proving that it was created out of a deeply perceived human need. Those who stake all on the dogma do so because it coheres with their belief, on other grounds, about the nature of the Universe.

The question which we must face, however, is whether the myth remains helpful in maintaining the values which it embodies. The tragic irony is that, while the Jesus of history was superbly free, the myth of Christ has become strait-jacketed into a religious formula. Thus the phrase 'Son of God' has become an offence (in the strict sense of the word) to the girl whose letter starts this section: there are many like her, and their number is growing. I have been criticized for throwing out the baby with the bathwater, but it seems to me that the mistake of orthodox defenders of Christianity is that in preserving, or attempting to preserve, the image of Christ which they have received, they are deterring a multitude of people who respond to the values which Jesus expressed, and with whom one feels he would have been more at home today than with the ecclesiastics and theologians. That in the name of a man as free as Jesus was, a religion should have grown up with such in-built restrictions and legalities as orthodox Christianity contains is one of the supreme tragic ironies of history and a blunt comment on human nature.

We may try – as some of those associated with non-church felt we should try – to 'rescue' the 'real' Jesus from the superimposed *persona*; but I believe that, for the present generation at least, this is an impossible task. The forces of orthodoxy, with their foothold in so many ledges – in schools through compulsory R.I. and worship, in factories, colleges and universities with their chaplaincies, through the mass media with their continual presentation of the either-or dilemma between Christianity and non-faith – are too established to prevent a type of in-fighting which would confuse, if not disgust, the non-theistic with whom they were ultimately attempting to communicate. The only answer for today is, as I wrote in my *Guardian* article, to drop any reference to 'Christ' and to 'Jesus', and to draw out the values thereafter to be expressed in human terms. It is difficult to believe that Jesus himself would have been worried about this in the slightest: if men are to be free, this must include freedom from the domination of his name.

One objection to the general non-theological approach advocated in this section, is that there is no justification for it in the life of Jesus. He was one to whom God was apparently real, to whom he could speak and with whom he could share his sense of mission. In addition, if the reference in Luke is any guide,[17] he attended worship regularly.

I am of course in no way committed to an acceptance of all that Jesus is alleged to have said and done as regulative for my life and thinking. I should not be expected to accept his concept of God if this is found inadequate, any more than many orthodox Christians do not accept his apparent treatment of mental disorders as being manifestations of devil-possession. Having said that, we can examine the suggestions made about Jesus to see if they are valid.

To claim that Jesus was a keen synagogue attender on the basis of one isolated text seems to me as offensive to the human intellect as is the justification of the papacy from two isolated texts in Matthew. It may have been the case; but we cannot be sure whether Luke was referring to just one period in Jesus's ministry, or that this had been Jesus's custom only up till then (but not afterwards). The fact that the story goes on to relate how Jesus was expelled from the synagogue may well be more significant for our understanding of his attitude than is the earlier comment. It is highly suggestive that we read no account of Jesus telling his followers, and the common people generally, that they should attend worship regularly, or more frequently than perhaps they did. We do read of his prophecies concerning the end of the Temple, and we have the mythical story of the

Transfiguration which seems to posit a warning against building any permanent memorial to Jesus. The conversation with the Samaritan woman[18] suggests a different type and place of worship than those to which we are now accustomed. The fact that Jesus's main conflicts were with those professional religious men who made their religion a way of life, dominated by regulations and their presence in religious buildings, gives added substance to the conviction that, if anything at all can be proved from the narratives as they stand, the tendency is away from, rather than towards, a building-dominated type of religion.

The evidence for Jesus's belief in what is traditionally termed a 'personal God' is, of course, undeniable: such references as his addressing God as 'Abba, Father' and the basing of many of his statements on the presupposition 'your heavenly father' are integral to his life. There are, however, three points to make, in ascending order of importance.

Firstly, it would be absurd to expect otherwise from one living in the first century of our era. Even supposing that he had possessed such a view of God as I outlined earlier, this would have meant little to his contemporaries, and to speak in that way would have been a deterrent to the acceptance of the basic elements of his message.

Secondly, it remains nevertheless true that the relationship between Jesus and God as described in the Gospels is a perfect example of what later writers have termed the 'I – thou' relationship. The mission to which he was dedicated received his total response: it was so complete that he refused to accept any of the restrictions imposed on ordinary people by the need to come to terms with, or submit to, the accepted authorities, rules, standards of the day. He was therefore responding, as only a completely free person can respond, to the 'ground of his being'. It possessed him utterly, so that in what he said and did men came to recognize 'God' acting and speaking. It seems that at times the evangelists themselves intended this interpretation. 'He who has seen me has seen the father', was his reply to one request that he should show them the father; 'I and the father are one'.[19] In other words, whatever men were looking for when they were looking for God, they had found in Jesus. I do not say that Jesus, or the evangelists, had necessarily worked it out in this way; I do suggest that for the interpretation of God and Jesus expressed in this section these words can be used as substantiation. In fact, on this interpretation, a non-theist could offer his assent, and the ground of difference between 'believers' and 'non-believers' would be revealed for what it is: *an illusion created by the blind literalism of theists on the one hand, and atheists on the other.*

Thirdly, whenever Jesus spoke of 'the Father', it was not in terms of 'pure' theology: it was 'applied', anchored in human response. His hearers give glory to the Father by letting their own light shine before men; the forgiveness of the Father is made possible only by human forgiveness; if men wish to avoid being judged, they must resist the impulse to judge others; as the Father gives good gifts, so 'whatever you wish that men would do to you, do so to them.' It is clear from a consideration of only the Sermon on the Mount (from which all these references are taken) that Jesus's teaching about the Father was related, closely and immediately, to human values and relationships. Thus we can, I think, justifiably say that at least the tendency of Jesus's teaching was not to postulate God as an entity extra to, over and above, the rest of life, but as one who met men in it. It is only one step further to suggest that life itself presents us with all that can or need be known about 'God'; and one further step, which I have advocated, to drop the word, though retaining the reality. This 'applied' theology of Jesus contrasts strongly, and strangely, with the 'pure' theology expounded by the orthodox of the Church. To be free from this was one of the freedoms which Jesus expressed; and in this, as in so much, we can share his attitude and the joy it brings.

One other question concerns the relationship between this image of Jesus and that of other leaders in human thought – founders of religions, philosophers, and so on: Moses, Buddha, Mohammed, Marx, or anyone who has set his seal on the personalities and characters of other people. Of course the relationship is close, and is being increasingly realized today. The indebtedness of modern Christians to the Jew, Buber, for their understanding of 'God', and to another Jew, Marx, for their interpretation of the tensions which are inevitable in an uneven economy, are two instances of this. Perhaps because there was that in Jesus which reached more deeply into what may loosely be called our humanity, his appeal throughout history has been broader than that of anyone else. But the difference is one of degree, not of kind.

The Body of Christ

Has the ongoing church, then, no part to play in meeting human needs according to this de-theologized view of Jesus? I wish to approach the answer to this by considering briefly two recently-published books: R. P. McBrien's *Do we need the Church*[20] and R. G. Jones' and A. J. Wesson's *Towards a Radical Church*.[21]

McBrien's book is interesting because, although a Roman Catholic, he rejects what he terms the 'pre-Copernican ecclesiology' which stated: 'All men should belong to the Church, because Jesus Christ founded the Church to make available for them the means of salvation.'[22] McBrien rejects this view on the grounds that it is God's Kingdom, and not the Church, which is the centre of history. Those in the Church are there by election, but they represent only one of the agencies of the Kingdom. Nevertheless, his conclusions provide a firmly positive answer to the question posed in the title. Firstly, Christians need the Church

> ... because it is the place where, by the choice of God, they 'have been called into the fellowship of His Son, Jesus Christ our Lord' ... (and) are called upon to become both sign and instrument of the Kingdom of God, i.e., of the human community as it emerges in time and history under the sovereignty, judgement and grace of the Gospel of Jesus Christ.
>
> Non-Christians, too, 'need' the Church. Indeed, the whole world 'needs' the Church, for the human community cannot long survive without fidelity to what is essentially human and criticism of what is fundamentally inhuman or antihuman. ... The Church must offer itself as one of the principal agents whereby the human community is made to stand under the judgement of the enduring values of the Gospel of Jesus Christ: freedom, justice, peace, charity, compassion, reconciliation...
>
> The human community needs a Church which proclaims without compromise the dignity and worth of every person, lest he be swallowed up in society's technological jaws. It needs a Church which reminds us all of the fragile character of our existence and of our history, which bridles our arrogance, strips us of our pretentious self-images. ... The world needs a Church which offers itself and all its resources as the embodiments of charity and as one of charity's principal instruments. The world, in the final accounting, needs a Church which, as a revolutionary community, never rests until the principles of the Gospel of Jesus Christ are everywhere realized and extended.

These are noble sentiments and, recognizing their source, bold. They are the most persuasive *apologia pro ecclesia* which I have come across: but they do not persuade me, for reasons which have been outlined already throughout this book. The objections can be reduced to four: firstly, once an organization is established, a disproportionate amount of the time and energy of its members must be expended on the organization. It may not be so much for members of the Roman Catholic as for members of the Free Churches; but the problem exists there too. I cannot see that there is any need for the existence of an organization to propagate goodness – for that, in plain terms, is what McBrien's arguments amount to. The various human needs he mentions, and the human values which he believes Christianity epitomizes and helps to preserve, can be established and preserved within existing structures by those who are determined that they shall be thrown into relief, and shall endure. Thus I am not in any sense a Manichee, or an ivory-tower idealist, as A. J. Wesson suggested in the letter referred to.[23] It may be that, where there is a particular human need, an *ad hoc* organization will have to be set up to meet that need. 'Shelter' is an example. In these circumstances, I could happily identify myself with the particular organization so long as the need lasted; but I would not do so if I were compelled thereby to give the impression that I were committed for life.

Secondly, the very existence of the Church encourages, if not induces, a large proportion of its devotees to think solely in terms of the Church, without reference to the human needs, or even to the 'mind of Christ'. In other words, a religious club is established which is for many members an end in itself. McBrien recognizes the danger of this in his strictures on pre-Copernican attitudes. In hoping he will change this, he is beating his head against the proverbial (and perhaps in his case literal) brick wall.

Thirdly, history stands starkly against the idealistic picture he gives. I do not deny that church members have contributed greatly to human progress in their individual lives. I suggest that almost all of these have done so without reference to their church affiliation, and many of them against the official counsel of their church. There were Christians in Germany who opposed Hitler; the Church generally was at best neutral. There are no doubt Christians in South Africa who oppose the equally detestable régime there; the Church itself is more for the régime than neutral. In fascist Spain the Church rubs its hands and hob-nobs with the authorities. Those few priests and laymen who speak out are rebuked by the Church. The same is reflected almost everywhere in the world. From Northern Ireland to Mexico, from Scarsdale in New York[24] to the Australian involvement in Vietnam, the Church as a body has been a political eunuch, and has lost any claim to be the leavening influence that McBrien claims it to be. What individuals there are who stand out from the church as representing the prophetic note can be matched from non-churchmen. It is impossible not to believe that the majority of churchmen who do so emerge are exponents of human values first and churchmen second; and that, whatever their religious beliefs or lack of beliefs, they would have made the same kind of stand.

Fourthly, because the Church (and McBrien himself) remain committed to a theological perspective, they are, if the letter at the start of this section is representative of the thinking of future generations, imprisoned within a theoretical system which is rapidly becoming a dead letter. And insofar (as I shall suggest in section four) as men today generally require the encouragement to stand on their own feet as masters of their fate, any such system must be viewed as obstructive to human progress. As McBrien himself summarizes Van Buren:

> 'God-talk' must be set aside. God, for us, is simply Jesus. And faith in Jesus is essentially an ethical stance. It means living as a 'man for others', living without regard to self, and being caught up in the contagion of Jesus' own freedom. In this view, the Church cannot be called the 'Body of Christ' in a descriptive sense. The theological and biblical designation is merely 'a reference to the historical perspective which the members presumably have in common, and it suggests the harmony that would exist between people who shared this perspective'.[25]

I would not go as far as Hamilton when he contends, 'The "Body of Christ" is irrelevant to the task of secular mission', since the group of people concerned, wherever they may be, will have their proportion of men and women with compassion, tolerance and dedication; and these will always be rare qualities among the human species. But I hold that within the 'Body of Christ' these qualities are tragically dissipated in a way which would be less likely to happen if they were totally secularized, or de-theologized. Consequently, McBrien's eloquent summary remains a series of well-phrased but ill-founded hopes, unrelated either to present facts or future probabilities.

The title of Jones' and Wesson's book promises much, but in the event turns out to be yet another castigation of the Church, together with the kind of blueprint for success which has been produced *ad nauseam* by SCM and other church conferences over

113

the past decade. In addition to the present church leaders, those whom this book hammers include Harvey Cox, Colin Morris and the 'political theologians'; Leslie Paul and other tidiers-up; liberal theologians from Schleiermacher to Tillich; the 'death of God' theologians; John Robinson, Charles Davis, myself and others of the non-church outlook; and, in some aspects, the Ecumenical Movement and localized moves towards church unity. Having demolished this lot by page 35, the authors then quote: 'If God be for us, who can be against us?' Two men plus God is obviously a majority in their estimation.

I must state emphatically that the ideas put forward in this book represent, in my view, the worst of every conceivable world. I state this not just because I am angered by this book in particular (though I am) but because it typifies the attitude of many of my former associates in the radical wing of the Church – an attitude of wanting to eat their cake and have it. The logical consequence of their viewpoint is to leave the existing Church and work outside it to construct one in their own image.

Our present argument, however, concerns their views on the necessity of the Church, the 'Body of Christ'. About this they are emphatic:

> It is amongst his (Jesus's) people that he becomes embodied in the world, so our response to him becomes expressed partly in a response to his people. One cannot be caught up in the ongoing work and purpose of Jesus Christ without being caught up with his people, the Church. . . .
>
> To believe in Jesus Christ is also to believe that a new, fresh, different, redeemed Church is already subtly in existence . . .
>
> So we suggest . . . for those who mean business about the renewal of the Church – a commitment to theology, (which) takes the world and its life with ultimate seriousness, for this is the arena in which God is acting.[26]

This approach does nothing but beg a number of vital questions. As a matter of fact, my life is now spent primarily with people who are certainly not 'caught up with the Church' yet are involved in what I should describe as the 'ongoing work of Jesus' – though neither I nor they so describe it: people who are attempting to bring tolerance, compassion, sympathy into the minds of students when contemplating the great human concerns of our time; men who are encouraging younger people to be themselves, to be creative, imaginative, employing to the full the

114

gifts with which they were born; above all, men and women who are playing their part in bringing a younger generation to a state of mind where they accept responsibility for themselves, their decisions, their relationships – in other words, to act maturely. If Jones and Wesson proceed to maintain that these people are members of this new Church which is subtly in existence then, again in the immortal words of Eric Morecambe, there's no answer to that. But I wonder of they are as *au fait* with the present human situation as they think.

The last paragraph quoted raises afresh (but not in a fresh way) the issue of the secular. There have been enough discussions of this in recent years not to require a long dissertation here. Harvey Cox[27] has already made clear that when he advocates secularization he does not mean secularism. Secularization is a process which began with the Renaissance but is reaching fruition only in our own time. It means, in the words of John Bennett, freedom from tribalisms, from obsessive ideologies, from the prejudices that are so familiar in our society, from secularism as a system.[28] Secularization is allied to pragmatism: it involves man in asking questions about himself, his background and environment; in finding his own motives for living, and making his own assessment of society and its needs. He will thus look for human rather than 'religious' values in living, and will depend on himself rather than on some 'other' power within him, or outside him.

Secularism, on the other hand, is closed and confining like any other system. It attempts to replace one set of imposed ideas with another, as anyone who has debated with members of the National Secularist Society will be aware. Harvey Cox states:

> Secularism . . . is the name for an ideology, a new closed world-view which functions very much like a new religion. . . . Like any other ism it menaces the openness and freedom secularisation has produced; it must therefore be watched carefully to prevent its becoming the ideology of a new establishment. It must be especially checked where it pretends not to be a world-view but nonetheless seeks to impose its ideology through the organs of the state.[29]

Non-secularization in Britain is exemplified by the compulsory school worship and religious instruction in our schools; by the seats obtained by certain bishops in the House of Lords (not that they do not necessarily deserve to be in that place on the grounds of their worth as human beings, but that they gain it automatically through their office as bishops); and in the religious rites which accompany the crowning of the monarch. Among Roman Catholics, it is evinced by the non-practice of birth control – where this is the consequence of obedience rather than any natural desire for a large family.

To replace a daily act of worship by the singing of the national anthem in schools, as has happened in the U.S.A., does nothing to help people become secular. In fact, both practices fall into the same category as the compulsory study of the thoughts of Chairman Mao, or of Karl Marx. The restrictions imposed on artists – writers, film-makers, painters – in the Soviet Union is an expression of one kind of secularism; the patriotic fervour of Americans in Vietnam another. Only when all absolutes are no longer imposed on members of these societies will we begin to understand to what heights of experience secularization can lead the human species. What is certain is that the attempt made by various Christians – radicals and others – to 'claim the world for God' and to see all good deeds as 'enhancing the ministry of Christ' is a potent means of preventing the secularization of man, apart from being unashamedly presumptuous. The following paragraph may be an improvement on a theology which views the world as inherently evil, and the Christian's purpose to be saved out of it, but the unabashed cocksureness of it gives it a malodour of its own:

> Christ is in politics when they lead in any way to His Kingdom. Christ is in economics when they manifest His healing, when they feed the hungry, clothe the naked. Christ is in the movements of men's minds, *whether Christian or not*, when they strive for a new internationalism, or for justice, or for peace, or for disarmament. Christ is in the call for honesty which millions today address to their politicians. . . .
> We can be with Him or against Him. We can look for Him or be blind to Him. The choice is ours. (italics mine – R.B.)[30]

If by Christ he means the myth which has survived the death of Jesus, symbolizing the many human qualities which Jesus showed in his life, then he is using a shorthand term which makes the paragraph tautologous. In other words, he is saying nothing, except, perhaps, expressing himself in favour of a better way of life for all – sentiments which are somewhat less than world-shaking. If, on the other hand, he is suggesting that because the western world has become so imbued with the spirit of Jesus that 'Christ-like' actions undertaken by non-believers indicate that they are really Christians in spite of their conscious beliefs, this is both arrogant and false.

Political Theology

Concentration on the concept of the Kingdom of God, as McBrien recommends, rather than on the Church, the body of Christ, has had the result of forcing some theologians to enter the world of political action. One of these is Harvey Cox, whose books *The Secular City* and *On Not Leaving it to the Snake*[31] demonstrate that in many ways he is akin to the Old Testament prophets in his concern that believers shall express their convictions about the human condition by being willing to act against any injustices which may exist in their own communities, even if such action involves them in standing out against the established order. We have seen a similar attitude in Britain in, for instance, the stand taken by many churchmen in favour of the Campaign for Nuclear Disarmament, and, more recently (and with perhaps less representation from the Church) against all-white South African cricket and rugby teams.

Cox has described how numerous churchmen in the United States became active 'futurists', inspired by men of the calibre of Martin Luther King. He writes with approval of the stand made by various Roman Catholic priests and laymen on the whole issue of race.[32] For example, when the Roman Catholic Bishop of Birmingham and Mobile told the nuns and priests who were marching in support of Luther King in Selma to go home and attend to 'God's business',

> . . . they not only refused to go but 300 of them signed a press statement spelling out their dissatisfaction with the archbishop and stating that they would return to Selma, or to other racial crisis spots, whenever Martin Luther King asked them to.

Similarly, when a Jesuit priest named Daniel Berrigan became co-chairman of an ecumenical group called Clergy Concerned About Vietnam and was ordered out to Latin America by the New York hierarchy for his pains, more than 1000 Catholics inserted an advertisement in the *New York Times* protesting about his banishment, and causing his recall. Some of the signatories were, like Berrigan, Jesuits – not normally noted for disobedience to their superiors.

Now everyone knows what many had long suspected: the day when the outrageous misuse of authority by the Catholic

Church would be met by silence and deference is gone forever.

(This is illustrated by certain opinions of catholic laypeople, as reported in *Newsweek* in March 1967. 70 per cent wanted to see the ban on birth control lifted, 59 per cent approved of abortion if the mother's life was in danger, 65 per cent wanted papal annulments of marriages ending in divorce [so that the innocent party could remarry] 48 per cent favoured marriage of priests.)

In the same article, Cox described how the need for social and political action had brought churchmen of all denominations into the public arena. He points out, however, that where unpopular political or social action was involved, 'a disproportionate number were denominational and interdenominational staff people, college and university chaplains'. It seems that the further a man can remove himself from the ecclesiastical machine, the freer he feels himself to be able to participate in direct action of some kind. This is illustrated in the community-organization work with which some of the American clergy are associated. Two non-churchmen, Saul Alinsky of the Industrial Areas Foundation, and Milton Kotler of the Institute for Policy Studies in Washington D.C., praise the churchmen 'because they are the only ones who have both a continuing existential interest in human community plus a fund of images to draw on'; but Cox argues that they probably do not appreciate how small a percentage of the total clergy are so involved.

My view is that churchmen who take such political action must be praised; but that they represent an era which will not survive, so that the grounds for what action they take must be restated. The Mississippi Delta Ministry, for instance, acknowledges this by implication when one of its reports describes how the Ministry 'emphasises meeting immediate human needs, community organization, economic development, education and public responsibility including voter education and registration. . . . Its staff members have been the catalyst in campaigns which have added 30,000 of Mississippi's new Negro voters to the registration lists'.[33]

Highly significant is the fact that this way-out Ministry has operated in the face of the bitter opposition of the Church in Mississippi. The same has been true of an equally praiseworthy 'direct action movement' – the Delano California Migrant Ministry, in which Roman Catholics, Protestants and Jews cooperate in fighting for the rights and status of farm workers. They have organized strikes, a nation-wide boycott of the company's product, and a 300-mile pilgrimage to gain sympathy for their actions. They attacked those in the church who condemned them for concerning themselves with matters other than 'spiritual' with their reply:

> We are not permitted to leave such considerations in the arena of pious generalities. They must be specific, and for us they have become burningly specific in the Delano grape strike.[34]

This kind of argument had been faced earlier by the Worker Priests in Paris, who had turned against the petit bourgeois class from which many of them originated, and which contained most of the city's practising Catholics. They became Communists, took part in peace marches, and two of their number were arrested for demonstrating against General Ridgway, the U.S. commandant to the NATO headquarters. But, as is written into the pages of history, the Church effectively castrated this movement, and although today fifty 'priests at work' are again labouring in French factories, a firmer hold is being kept on them, and they are compelled to maintain a close link with official Catholicism in their area. *Absit omen.*

The same frustration has been expressed by Horst Symanowsky of the Gossner Mission. Writing in *Over the Bridge* he said:

> I understand the theological students who came out of the factory to me and said that they did not want to study theology any more; *this* world could not be won by preaching or witness. Religious trimmings as a means of communication are out of date. How can the person who has been thrown out of almost all traditions still approve the religious one? It becomes ballast to be thrown overboard as soon as possible. We should recognise that the world has grown up.[35]

My purpose in quoting these examples is not to belabour a point which has already been – I hope – firmly established in these pages, but to indicate that, though the church has its quota of political revolutionaries, their effectiveness begins where they leave behind the distinctively 'religious' element. When Wilfred Wooller criticizes those parsons who are determined to demonstrate against South African sportsmen, and advises them to return to their 'spiritual pursuits', he epitomizes the brake which 'pure' religion must always put on 'applied' religion. (Not that

I'm conceding to Mr. Wooller any right to be speaking for the spiritually-minded of the land.

Harvey Cox's political theology is both a challenge and a contrast to most expressions of Christianity today. He states emphatically:

> Future church historians will certainly notice that the major religious figures of our era, the saints of the twentieth century, achieved their sainthood mainly in political disobedience.[36]

Cox himself is refreshingly free from ecclesiasticism, and I feel that he would have been a valuable addition to the staff at Woolwich. One of our weaknesses, on reflection, lay in the fact that there was nowhere in the local political scene where we were positively active. I think we made our presence felt on a number of issues; but we needed a member on the local council, if not as a local M.P., in order to be able to do more than comment on local issues from the sidelines. Cox's sense of commitment – illustrated in his continual help with the Cape Cod experiment – is a rebuke to any amateurish approach to such issues: he realizes, with Lenin, that one cannot make an omelette without breaking eggs.

Yet in the end he is, I believe, doomed to be superceded. A sentence on the last page of *On Not Leaving it to the Snake* illustrates why I feel this:

> God's main intention is not the renewal of the church but the renewal of the world.

In that sentence is epitomized the strength and weakness of Cox's position. His strength lies in his lack of commitment to the ecclesiastical; and there should be no under-estimation of the boldness of this stand. In a country which can still boast church attendances which make those in Britain seem virtually non-existent in comparison, he has stood back and, like the prophet of old, condemned the feasts and sacrifices and called for justice and mercy. This is good, and may well be *at the moment* the best that can be looked for on the American religious scene. His weakness, however, lies in his continuing lip-service to an outdated myth. The world certainly needs to be changed; but if the perspective is that of the attitude of 'God', it will be written off by the new generations for whom this is a myth which no longer relates to their condition, or their needs. Something much bolder is needed – something which eats into the heart of the existing situation.

120

I conclude, therefore, that the concept of the 'Body of Christ' is one that should be quietly laid to rest. There are so many different motivations and viewpoints represented by those who claim this title for themselves that it tends to be meaningless. Equally significant, there are sufficient people who make no claim to the title yet display some of the qualities of those who do to blur any distinctions implied in the phrase. If we follow McBrien and think, as he suggests Jesus thought, in terms of the Kingdom of God rather than of the Church, we are left with another question-begging phrase which may be subjectively helpful to those for whom the concept of God is still real, but which is useless for that growing number to whom it is not.

What none of the books mentioned in these last few pages can do, any more than any book written in the context of religious convictions can do (defining 'religious' here as including a belief in the 'supernatural' as earlier defined), is to speak to the girl whose letter was quoted on page 83. The question which Christians will raise is, who is right and who is wrong: will the Christian view prevail, or hers? My own conviction is that she speaks for her own, and every subsequent, generation, unless man is going at some stage to slip back into the superstitions of his ancestors. Recommendations about how to live will, I believe, be discarded if they are offered within a 'religious' or 'supernatural' context. Only intrinsically can human values hope to gain acceptance in the future. I do not deny that the Christian faith confirms some, if not many, of these values; and that among any average congregation there will be a proportion of people who are deeply concerned about them. What I fear is that with the rejection of the doctrines which is happening now there will be a tendency to condemn also the values – a case of guilt by association. The greatest task facing man today is to express these values in terms which people can understand and accept.

With considerable trepidation, I shall attempt, in the final section, a preliminary statement of these values.

Section Four

HUMAN VALUES

IN his *Theology for Radical Politics*, Michael Novak gives his first chapter the title 'The Inadequacies of the Old Order'. In this he states what has been the theme of this book;

> The quest for human values in our society . . . has been radically secularised. It has moved outside the churches. If one wishes to be radically religious in our society – that is to say, radically committed to a vision of human brotherhood, personal integrity, openness to the future, justice and peace – one will not, commonly, seek an ecclesiastical outlet for one's energies. One will, instead, create one's own symbols for community and integrity, and work through secular agencies for social and political reforms. The saints of the present (and perhaps of the future) are no longer ecclesiastics and churchgoers or even, necessarily, believers in God. The saints of the present are, in the words of Albert Camus, secular saints. [1]

I believe this to be a correct assessment of the situation and, this being so, feel that we should be wiser to drop the word 'religious' in this connection, since this word is redolent of so many different interpretations. If to feel, and seek to express, a deep concern about the human situation, about the meaning of existence, and about the nature and destiny of man, is to be religious, then what I now have to say is in that category. But insofar as what I shall say demands the rejection of any received symbols, absolutes, myths, including (and especially) those traditionally described as 'religious' – God, the supernatural, anything or anyone 'other than' human – I prefer that what I state shall be considered an attempt only to put into words those human values which seem to me to spring *a priori* from the human situation. The fact that some may not recognize these values as elemental must be acknowledged; but they can only be stated in the hope that they express something integral to human nature which will therefore evoke a response in the minds of the present and any future generation.

The purpose of life can be summed up in one word: fulfilment. This means that man is born to achieve his potential – physically, mentally, imaginatively, and in terms of his relationships with others. In turn, this implies that those institutions of society which do not enable people so to grow must be reshaped until they do; and any facets of society which militate directly against such growth must be destroyed. Julian Huxley has written about this with his customary eloquence. I should emphasize that in the quotation which follows I dislike his use of the phrase 'humanist religion': both words seem to me to beg more questions than they clarify. I prefer the neutral phrase which is the title of this section; but with the sentiments I have no quarrel:

> A humanist religion will certainly do something new – it will assign a high religious value to the increase of scientifically based knowledge: for it is on knowledge and its applications that anything which can properly be called human advance or progress depends. It will also assign a high value to the creative imagination and the works of art and beauty and significance which it produces; for it is they which are the highest expressions of the spirit of man.
>
> As regards the individual, it will, like the ancient Greeks, stress *excellence*. But as complementary to this, it will go further than the Greek principle of moderation: nothing too much – and will make psychological integration and total wholeness an essential aim, and in some sense the equivalent of the state of salvation in Christian terminology.[2]

So far as social fulfilment is concerned, Huxley writes:

> The humanist goal must therefore be, not Technocracy, nor Theocracy, nor the monolithic and authoritarian State, nor the Welfare State, nor the Consumption Economy, but . . . a society which provides opportunities for education, for adventure and achievement, for co-operating in worthwhile projects, for meditation and withdrawal, for self-development and unselfish action.

Clearly, all these suggestions are at this stage no more than invitations to discussion. We must consider the concept of fulfilment more fully, first in relation to the individual, and then in terms of society – while recognizing that these two are interdependent, and that any distinction of this kind is consequently artificial.

124

a. *Personal Fulfilment*

Three factors seem to be of paramount importance here.

1. *Personal identity*

'Know thyself' remains the first commandment for anyone seeking personal fulfilment. How can he be fulfilled until he is aware of who the person is that is to be fulfilled? Yet even to state the problem in those words indicates the difficulty: how can one be both subject and object of one's own awareness? If we could, like the Ka of Gifford Hilary as described by Dennis Wheatley, somehow withdraw from ourselves and at the same time survey ourselves, this might be an easier task to achieve. How much, in any case, *are* we ourselves, and how much do we *become* ourselves? How much do innate temperament, abilities, personality affect the choices we make, the way we proceed through life, the identity, or identities, which we choose to assume, and how much do our choices qualify our personalities? Is any person static? Is there any living creature that is not undergoing the process of change? Michael Novak says:

> We make ourselves who we are. Either that or we merely drift and let our parents, our teachers, our society, our peers make us into what they want us to be. It is a terrible fate not to have chosen one's own identity; a terrible fate to have been made, like an object, by others.[3]

This interplay between innate and social tendencies cannot be avoided by any human being. However, from an early age the individual can be encouraged to analyse his own attitudes and reactions in any situation, to assess how far he is responding to stimuli provided by earlier social frameworks – the home and family, friends and relatives – and how far he is seeking an objective answer to the problem before him. When experiencing a sense of guilt he will ask himself what exactly makes him feel this; when filled with awe or wonder, he will be encouraged to ask why he feels as he does, and what this tells him about his own particular human qualities; when faced with a decision, he will learn to distinguish between blind adherence to the choice made by others before him, and his own conclusions – affected, of course, by those of others, but not determined by them. So he can be encouraged to act only when he reaches the conclusion which satisfies him, and for which he can give a satisfactory reason.

In the process, he will learn to view himself not as white, or

English, or working-class, or Christian, or communist: he will recognize himself for what he is – a human being, unique in that there is no replica of himself in the universe, but sharing with all other human beings basic needs, hopes, fears, desires, aims and motives. 'I am that I am' means every living person; so the human race is at the same time a collection of unique individuals and a multitude sharing the common gift of humanity. This is the only viable basis of morality. When a white South African demands to know why his black colleague should receive as good an education, should live in as comfortable a house, and do the same type of work for the same amount of money, as he does, the only answer required is: because he, like you, is a human being. The very fact that the United Nations Organisation felt it necessary to issue its Universal Declaration of Human Rights is a proof that hitherto men have not adequately reflected on the implications of this. But the time must come when all men everywhere are led so to reflect, so that all enter into their reward: the inheritance, in full measure, of their own humanity.

2. *Maturity*

If man is to capture and maintain this viewpoint, he must accept his own self-responsibility; in other words, he must be mature. In Emerson's words,

> And we are now men, and must accept in the highest mind the same transcendent destiny; and not minors and invalids in a protected corner, not cowards fleeing before the revolution, but guides, redeemers, benefactors, obeying the almighty effort, and advancing on Chaos and the Dark.

This sentiment cuts right across any sense of reliance upon 'God' to see us through, whether expressed in the words of Augustine – 'Thou hast made us for Thyself . . .' – or in the 'modern' words, 'He holds the whole world in His hand'. Man cannot abdicate responsibility in this way; and for too long his maturity has been retarded by this concept.

What in practice does it mean? It means surrendering the bovine attitude which has allowed the few to bear the headaches while the many grumble about their decisions. It means that people must be more willing to accept responsibility for their own destinies, and for the part they play in the destinies of others. It involves a growing self-reliance, tolerance, assurance. It means increasingly abandoning the pillars and props afforded to men by principles and moral absolutes. Men must be encouraged to

126

think problems through for themselves, and not to feel that they themselves are being belittled if somebody else disagrees with them. Thus, a maturity of outlook will make possible a greater depth of relationship with a wider range of people. Too often people choose their friends and associates from amongst those whose mental processes are like their own; this too easily – and sometimes fatally – divides men into segregated groups which find it difficult if not impossible to communicate with members of other groups. The mature man will be at ease in any company – or almost any company – since this company contains human beings like himself who, when the outer crust comprising the labels and name-tags is removed, share many of his own deepest concerns.

I recognize that maturity of personal relationships does not mean that every person one gets to know must enter into the 'I – thou' category. Most people will be fortunate if they can name twenty people in their lives with whom the intensity of relationship so described is possible. But, as Harvey Cox has argued,[4] this does not mean that most people must be relegated to the 'I – it' category; there is a middle way – that of 'I – you', in which, while one does not become deeply involved, the fact that any encounter between people is between two human beings is not lost sight of. We do not choose 'I – thou' relationships: we find them happening because of who we are and who the other person is. However, we can choose to make 'I – it' relationships into 'I – you': and the extent to which people generally are anxious and willing to do this is one of the signs of their maturity.

Here is an example of the type of relationship, or non-relationship, which must disappear with human maturity:

> A 25-year-old coloured man was attacked and stabbed in a South London back street today. He slumped unconscious to the ground from loss of blood and later surgeons fought for four hours to save his life . . .
> Mrs. Y. Z. of XXX Road was woken by shouts and screams at the time of the attack. She said today: 'I could hear shouting and screaming. I didn't think of looking out of the window. It's something you just get used to. You mind your own business. I went back to sleep.'[5]

I view this attitude as primarily an indication of immaturity – the immaturity of the child who is afraid to venture beyond the immediate circle of his family, or the adult who mixes only with the small circle of friends whom he has known for years.

Clearly, the type of maturity I am advocating demands a willingness to take trouble with people for their own sakes; in other words, it requires sympathy, compassion, understanding. Put another way, man must expect to have to suffer, for, as Unamuno wrote,

> ... suffering is the substance of life and the root of personality, and suffering is universal. Suffering is that which unites all us living beings together; it is the universal or divine blood that flows through us all. That which we call Will, what is it but suffering?

Suffering and maturity: bearing the burdens of the world he has inherited – these are the requirements if man is to achieve his birthright. The existentialists would contend that it is only at the moment when he makes decisions for himself, in relation to his own destiny, that he becomes truly human. It was only when in his cell, awaiting the carrying out of the death sentence, that Bonhoeffer discovered how useless were all the supports which had sustained him until then. 'God', the Gospel, the 'Word' – all fell away and left him exposed to the alien blasts, to bear the burden himself. Men shrink from this, but they must be encouraged to view such responsibility as of the stuff of humanity, within the context of the tensions, the problems, the 'causes for concern' which are perpetually around us, and which most people too easily leave to others, or 'them', to resolve.

MORAL ABSOLUTES

We have already considered the prop of God; at this point we must consider that other prop which makes life easier for most people, and yet prevents them from achieving maturity – the plank of moral absolutes. While these have been affirmed in relation to religions other than Christian, and without reference to any religion at all, in the present context these must be considered only insofar as they allegedly spring from a Christian viewpoint.

As I write, my children, absent from school for a half-term breather, are watching a schools broadcast on television. I hear the voice of one participant emanating through: 'Let us consider the Christian view of this problem.' I do not know what the problem is, nor do I care: there is no Christian view of any problem – only the attitude developed over a number of years in a particular culture under certain influences. The plaintive utterance of a committee on which I was speaking about censorship illustrates this attitude: 'Haven't we as Christians anything distinctive to say on this matter?' Why on earth anyone should want to have something distinctive to say on any problem is beyond my comprehension: the whole attitude reeks of the legalist who enters the conference chamber with his options firmly closed. He is like the trade unionist who remarked, 'Certainly we will let this matter go to arbitration; but we will not change our minds or our demands.' It is an approach which appeals to the man of small mind, who can avoid the responsibility of working through an issue for himself, and fall back on some principle handed to him by his elders and peers. The issue under discussion never becomes part of his own experience: it is just one other problem to receive the treatment; principles triumph over persons.

The most blatant example of this in modern times is the Papal Encyclical on Birth Control. This profoundly dehumanized document exemplifies a world and thought-form which must be destroyed if man is to inherit his birthright. It is sad enough that a man who was heralded into power with so many fanfares as a reformer should so rapidly and so convincingly expose his inadequacy for the role; even sadder is that millions of Roman Catholics, each knowing more about the problems under discussion than the Pope will ever know, should obey him. Their conditioning resembles that of the South African non-whites, reared from birth to an ignoble subservience. What makes the papal attitude laughable as well as contemptible is the apparent reluctance of Jesus to make any kind of absolutist statements. We will search the Gospels in vain for any declaration on human rights, denunciation of nationalism, racialism, or any other ism, or pronouncements on any other 'cause'.[6]

I accept that, on the argument presented in the last section, dependence on the New Testament as justification of any viewpoint is an unjustifiable use of the documents concerned; so I shall test the concept of maturity I have expressed in relation to the sphere *par excellence* in which moral absolutes are introduced: sex. What does it mean to be mature in sexual behaviour? How far should sexual relationships be governed by inherited rules, and how far are they the preserve only of the couple concerned, for which criticism from outside is a presumptuous imposition?

There are two initial considerations which will affect any decision on this matter. Firstly, the question to be borne in mind is not, How much is allowed? or How far can we go? It is What is of worth? Thus, secondly, we shall be motivated by

John Robinson's suggestion that when making up our minds about a male/female relationship our concern should be with the depth, rather than the extent, of the relationship.

My own upbringing, like that of most people of my background, was more concerned with the issue of extent than with the question of depth. Teaching on sexual morality which I received from various quarters had as its key the concept that full sexual experience was the preserve only of the married couple: biological need must be subservient to sociological custom. Sex was spoken of as a solemn process, sexual experience a responsible activity; I recall reading or hearing little on the pleasure, or fun, of sex.

For my own part I believe that heavy petting, which stops just short of copulation, is at once morally and psychologically more disturbing (and possibly no less intimate) than complete intercourse, which may be undertaken by mature persons with a natural joy not unmixed with reverence.

It would be illuminating to discover how many marriages have been ruined because of the in-built, long-sustained resistance to intercourse which such a habit must frequently create. I am well aware that we must not underestimate the dangers of laxity. The latest figures for venereal disease are disturbing and permissiveness may give *carte blanche* to those who see their partners solely in terms of genitals as well as to the Casanovas, sadly incapable of maintaining a deep relationship, who have always been with us. But I cannot see that pre-marital intercourse is of itself to be in all circumstances condemned; it may sometimes be psychologically beneficial and the expression of a mature love.

What then shall be said about post-marital fidelity? Is not the commandment not to commit adultery an absolute? To view it in this general way seems to me to be taking a naive view of the situation. There is no absolute adultery; there are many different people who for a variety of reasons have sexual relationships in a variety of ways, not all physical, with someone other than their spouse.

It is entirely right that the new marriage act should no longer allow adultery as a ground for divorce. Each human situation is different and it is not for me to pronounce on any situation other than my own. One Australian psychologist affirmed in 1968 that while adultery can destroy some marriages, in others it can be a strengthening factor bringing the married pair back with renewed interest in each other. He acknowledged that the marriage would have to be of mature people for this to be so; but stated that he knew some marriages which had been *saved* by adultery.

I do not want to be misunderstood here. *I am not advocating adultery* but am suggesting that in our assessment of its rightness or wrongness we shall not appreciate the human issue at stake if we approach the question on the basis of the attitude: all adultery is wrong because it contravenes some moral code. Any such code is nothing more than the customs of a particular society in a certain place and situation. What they decide to be necessary for the preservation of that society may well be the right decision in those circumstances. The trouble is that the ethical practices of one generation or society become the moral principles of the next, often made absolute by the affirmation that this is 'God's law'. In changing circumstances and conditions, these principles may well remain like an appendix in a body which has outgrown the need for it. Again I don't want to be misunderstood. I do not affirm that principles inherited in this century from the past are necessarily irrelevant to our age. I am simply stating that they are not relevant now *just because* they were two thousand, or four thousand, years ago, in vastly different circumstances. If we are to take hold of and express our maturity, we shall act in accordance with our own assessment of what is good or bad for society as we now experience it. We may well reach the same conclusions as did our ancestors. But it will be our decision, not theirs.

Of course many acts of adultery are expressions of selfishness and greed, and are committed with an immature disregard for the consequences. But there may be circumstances in which adultery could not be condemned out of court. There may be something 'wrong' with the marriage that requires this (though I am not conceding this): but in that case the task of anyone concerned must be to make a sympathetic analysis of the cause rather than the symptoms. My own view is that, provided nobody is hurt in the process (and I appreciate that this is a major proviso) it would be an impertinence on my part to criticise extra-marital sexuality. I would accept that for some people it is possible to love more than one member of the opposite sex at the same time; and that in those circumstances the person or persons concerned must accept responsibility for their actions. It is their duty not to cause grief or pain to others; and this implies that restraint, rather than free expression, may be required of them. Otherwise, what they do is their concern alone.

Would this not be a dangerous doctrine to proclaim? How

would children, or adolescents, react to such an approach? Obviously, with young children there needs to be hard-and-fast rules. I would not dream of encouraging my children, now bordering on adolescence, to work these problems out for themselves at this stage. For the present, in their state of immaturity, the rules (on whatever subject – sex is not a major source of anxiety to them yet) are laid down, though this does not mean that they are not at the same time explained. But as the children mature, I should be failing in my duty as a parent if I did not encourage them to think more deeply and more positively about rule-governed behaviour. Norman Williams has suggested that there are critical periods in any child's life when 'there may be crucial or optimal times for the achievement of developmental tasks, and, . . . if this period is missed, the task will be achieved only with very great difficulty, or not at all.'[7] If this is so, then it is the parent's or teacher's responsibility to be aware of the situation, and to be ready to take the opportunity thus provided of leading the child or adolescent to a new understanding of himself, and a deeper awareness of the responsibilities, for himself and for others, which he carries. Williams' conclusion on the matter of moral development seems to me to express the right attitude:

> There can be no question of anyone concerned with child care, or education, abdicating responsibility for moral development. . . . In these activities we may advance, or retard, the child's moral development; and we educate more frequently by what we do and what we are than by what we say . . . One does not say 'I shall make this child introject this quality or that attitude'. The child does not consciously select a particular adult as a model. We are furthering or hindering a child's moral progress every time we foster his self-respect by giving real responsibility, or remain uninterested in trivial problems that loom large to him, or make arbitrary decisions overriding his developing ability to think for himself. We are all moral educators, whether we like it or not.[8]

3. Creativity

This would seem to be the most natural expression of human maturity. Michael Novak writes:

> The universe in which we live often seems impersonal, indifferent, hostile, and even cruel. Yet our experience

within it often fills us with reconciliation, with a sense of unity and peace, with a profound stirring of ecstasy and the desire to create.[9]

Unfortunately (for the present discussion) he then proceeds to relate this to the concept of God:

> Man is coming to life again; taste and see that the taste of life is sweet! When man regains his roots in nature, the God immanent in nature courses through his consciousness again. The dead God rises. The arrowhead breaks through into a new, creative, period.[10]

I prefer simply to affirm that the faculty to create, to produce order out of chaos, to bring into existence that which previously did not exist – a song, a poem, a tune, a building, a picture – represents man the inheritor of the wisdom of the universe. As Emerson wrote:

> A man is the whole encyclopedia of facts. The creation of a thousand forests is in one acorn, and Egypt, Greece, Rome, Gaul, Britain, America, lie folded already in the first man.

If from the earliest years our children can be brought gradually to understand what this implies, and encouraged to use their skills and imaginations creatively, expressing themselves as profoundly as they are able, we may begin to see a *human* society worthy of the best that is inherent in that epithet.

Of course I am aware of the many influences in society which, directly or indirectly, deter people from entering into their inheritance. From the time when he enters a secondary school, if not earlier, the child is confronted with the proposition (which asserts itself through the system, despite any antipathy toward it on the part of any particular teacher) that learning, the use of the imagination, hard and dedicated work, are not ends in themselves but society's requirements before granting the necessary qualifications for a particular post. Thus, by the time he is eighteen, the student will find it almost impossible not to judge any work he undertakes by its importance to him in his career, or in terms of the extra stipend which any resultant qualification might bring him. He is already on the way to becoming a stereotyped citizen, a bloodless commuter, a mass-produced specimen mouthing only those viewpoints which gain general acceptance among his colleagues and peers. The sense of life as an experiment, as an adventure, as a series of explorations to which the individual can

133

render the best of himself can easily be stifled: I have seen the end-product a thousand times as technical students, encouraged by their lecturers (in turn encouraged by academic boards and industrial overseers) sink uncomplainingly into their prepared grooves. (No wonder many of them have highly active sex lives: it is one area where every encounter is an adventure, and for which they do not even have to get out of bed.)

Is this to continue to be the lot of the majority of mankind? Is Tennyson's mood of aspiration to be the preserve only of the idealistic few – who probably by definition opt out of any contemporary rat race? –

> I am part of all that I have met:
> Yet all experience is an arch wherethro'
> Gleams that untravelled world, whose margin fades
> For ever and for ever when I move ...

Bertrand Russell was quite certain that, provided the nuclear holocaust could be avoided (and there are several other grim facts of life which could be added, all with their distinctive threats to the future survival of man) the innate creative capacities of most people may well be tapped:

> In such a world as men could now make, if they chose, it could be freely creative in the framework of our terrestrial existence. In recent times, knowledge has grown so fast that its acquisition has been confined to a tiny minority of experts. . . . We are suffering from undigested science. But in a world of more adventurous education this undigested mass would be assimilated and our poetry and art could be enlarged to embrace new worlds to be depicted in new epics. The liberation of the human spirit may be expected to lead to new splendours, new beauties and new sublimities impossible in the cramped and fierce world of the past. [11]

This is a proud vision: must it remain no more than a gleam in the eye of the romantic? I am myself ambivalent about it. I recognize the increasing utilitarianism in some aspects of society: the reduction of all values, as in the world of advertising, to the monetary worth of the area under consideration; the repetitiveness of may facets of modern living; the indifference, bordering on contempt, of many people towards any of their fellows who are not close replicas of themselves in their attitudes and behaviour. At the same time I realize that the ancient gods are dead; outworn slogans and attitudes (like patriotism, for example, or class) are slowly becoming matters of history rather than sociology; so that more children than ever before can start life in this country with the sense that this is a brave new world into which they are embarking. If we seize the opportunity, (and there have been moments of crisis in history, akin to those in the life of any individual, when opportunities for rapid progress have presented themselves, some of which, as at the Renaissance, were accepted), there seems no reason to reject Russell's prophecy as a piece of hopelessly sentimental idealism.

4. *Quality, not quantity*

This is a contrast which has become almost a cliché, and I shall not pursue it at length. Clearly, to say that what a man is is more important than what he has is to make a value judgement. It cannot be proved empirically: it remains almost a metaphysical proposition, and can be demonstrated only by example. If what I am affirming is truly integral to the human condition, people will learn that success cannot be achieved for the price of a packet of toothpaste, and will reject any expression of values which attempts to persuade them otherwise. They will reject any suggestion that a cup of something or a packet of something else will open the gateway to gracious living. They will realize that the world of culture and the arts will not reveal its secrets just by the payment of a small deposit. Quality cannot be bought, but it can be earned; and sooner or later any man, if he is truly human, will learn to recognize and appreciate it when he sees it. When he does this, and wholeheartedly pursues it for himself, a man can know that he is worthy of his ancestors, and one of whom his descendants may speak with pride.

Social Fulfilment

It will take more space than is available here to outline adequately what is meant by social fulfilment. All we can do – or need do, since there is a multitude of writers in this field – is to outline what the ideal community will contain; indicate some of the barriers to this in society today; and consider how men may best bring about the society of which they dream.

A community may be defined as a group of free, independent people who relate to each other at various levels of experience. Each member will be dependent on the rest of the community for the fulfilment of many of his needs: in a large community like a town, basic physical needs like food, water, housing, will be so met. In the smaller environmental communities other needs will be met: the need to communicate by language; the need to have certain values; the need for love, for compassion, for caring; in the smallest and most intimate community – the family – the needs of sex, parenthood and home-making. Within these communities, the individual has a responsibility to give as well as to receive; and if the community is to be healthy, in the sense of wholeness, there are two functions in particular which any person has to perform, irrespective of particular contributions he may make because of his distinctive personality or gifts: understanding, and criticism. Unless the members show the first of these, any community will become cold, impersonal, a series of isolated cells; unless there be criticism, injustices or deficiencies will go uncorrected. Both of these can mean the death of a community – the one by neglect, the other by stagnation. As Michael Novak puts it:

> A community that lacks reconciliation destroys itself through fratricide. A community that lacks prophetic criticism destroys itself through immobility.[12]

I shall illustrate the need for each of these from three areas which constitute communities of widening dimensions: the family, the urban environment, and the world scene.

The Family

The increased mobility of modern life has put a strain on family ties beyond any experienced by our ancestors. Until this century it was normal for people to spend their whole lives surrounded by members of their family, since few moved away from the area where they were born. It is still so, to a certain extent, in village communities in this country. But as the population is caught up in urban and industrial development, sons and daughters move away and, with the economic pressures of modern life forcing many women to go out to work, opportunities for all the family to meet are often rare.

Even where the members of a family see much of each other, this does not necessarily mean that the compassion that each needs is always being shown. The natural barrier between the generations is one factor here; another is the lack of communication between husband and wife, which, if not more prevalent today than in earlier times, is a factor in the breakdown in many marriages. Erich Fromm argued:

> People are indoctrinated to think that if two people are married, have children, don't quarrel, the man isn't un-

faithful – which these days seems a rather rare phenomenon – then they love each other, because they have been told that, provided all these things are present, it is love. What you might find in reality is that they feel nothing. They have a kind of friendly feeling you might have towards a stranger . . . I have seen many couples who have talked, who have really talked to each other for the first time, *only* when they talk divorce.

I am not discussing whether the family has declined in importance as a community within which people today have the needs satisfied which are traditionally associated with it. Ronald Fletcher argues convincingly that it has not declined[13] and I see no reason to reject his conclusions. The issue is that of deciding, where these needs are not being met, why this is so, and what can be done to restore them, or to ensure that fewer families in the future do not suffer the same fate.

Urban life

Schopenhauer suggested that people were like hedgehogs: uncomfortable and pricking each other when close together, and miserable when apart. Perhaps one of the reasons why cities are often condemned today as depersonalized places is that people are being too closely packed together, so that their psychological withdrawal becomes a defence mechanism. Whatever be the reason, Julian Huxley's condemnation must be faced:

> City life today is leading to mass mental disease, to growing vandalism and possible eruptions of mass violence.[14]

It could be that the mental disease is, ironically enough in a vast conurbation, the result of loneliness – the consequence of feeling that nobody cares. Richard Hoggart has described[15] his own boyhood in Leeds when, in what we should today describe as a slum, people communicated with each other, and if one was sick the others would know, and would unite to help as best they could. It is often affirmed that on modern housing estates nobody cares, the individual is not missed if he does not appear for some days, and there is seldom any natural meeting place for the members of the community. J. B. Priestley has described this unambiguously:

> Modern suburban young wives have to keep paying visits to the doctor, not because they are really sick in body, but because they are a trifle sick in mind. The trouble is that

> they feel depressed, dreary, and terribly lonely. . . . There is
> something thin, brittle, mechanical about their life. It lacks
> richness, human variety, sap and juice, just because it has no
> real social background. . . . The people do not really *belong*
> to the place they are in, but are camping in it. They are no-
> mads without a tribe.[16]

If that last sentence is true, then we are in danger of entering
into the worst of all possible worlds: being surrounded by people
without all the therapeutic benefits that this should bring;
living in a sense of isolation without the tranquillity which those
who choose to live in, say, rural surroundings can expect to
experience.

How far vandalism and violence are caused by cities is perhaps less demonstrable. Nicholas Taylor argued in *Help* magazine
that the increased vandalism on housing estates resulted primarily because the estates were not made responsible for their
own maintenance. He adds:

> It is interesting that the worst vandalism can be
> observed on those estates . . . where the architects have
> followed the fashionable middle-class aesthetic of the
> 'neo-slum' – dark brick and rough concrete, tough materials
> for tough areas, the equivalent of corporal punishment
> (with similar counter-productive results).[17]

For a discussion of the cause-and-effect relationship between the
city and violence, I refer the reader to Desmond Morris's
The Human Zoo.[18] I'm not sure that I accept the argument that
violence is the direct consequence of people's living too close
together. I saw more violence during my four years in Hereford –
hardly a densely-packed city – than during six years in south-east
London. It could be that there is today less sense of adventure, of
exploration, less opportunity for self-expression, than obtained a
century or more ago. But, in bemoaning, as we tend to do, the
present age in this connexion we forget, on the one hand, that we
read only of the few in the past who were able to satisfy their
thirst for adventure and self-expression while the many worked in
drudgery; and, on the other hand, that, while it may still constitute a risk to walk alone in one or two parts of a few of our
cities late at night, a century ago this was true of most parts of
most cities; it therefore seems to me quite false to write our age
off as one of distinctive violence.

However, problems remain in our systems, and again they

relate to the question of human values, and how they can be instilled. How shall people gain such depth of character that they will desire communication at more than surface level with their neighbours, their colleagues, their associates? On what basis will people be led to reject 'I – it' in favour of 'I – you'?

World tensions

The problems on the world scene are most blatant of all; yet they have emerged within a situation pregnant with possibilities for the expression of the values I have outlined earlier. Increased mobility has brought together races and nations to an extent beyond the imaginations of our ancestors. The one world of the seers and prophets is potentially a reality. The opportunities now exist for different peoples to enrich their own cultures by insights gleaned from others. The areas of relationships have widened immeasurably, and new and original concepts from traditions different from one's own are now more readily available. Cross-fertilization of many kinds is possible; it appears that the stage is set for man to enter into a new phase of civilization.

Yet somewhere along the road the process seems to have turned sour. Instead of rejoicing in new ideas, new types of creativity, different personalities with presuppositions which contrast with their own, there has been, on the part of a large proportion of the population, a reluctance to join the wider scene. Instead of welcoming those who bring new attitudes about the human situation, doors – figurative and literal – have been closed to them. Insularity has manifested itself, not unmixed with selfishness. The rich white west has closed its eyes to the needs of the Third World. In place of compassion in the shape of food, tractors or technicians, excesses of income over expenditure have been spent on weapons of destruction so potentially devastating that the continuing existence of man on this planet rests on the coolness and sense of responsibility of a handful of their number. In the nations' processes of getting rich and powerful more quickly than their neighbours, the balance of nature has been broken, and pollution of the countryside, of the air, of the rivers and lakes has become a Fact of Life. In relating all this to attitudes in Britain, Colin Morris writes:

> Whilst fifty-five million people starve to death each year, the *Unpoor* squandor astronomic sums on advertising to tickle the jaded appetites of their overstuffed people. Britain spends six times more on advertising than overseas aid.

Her people must be enticed to eat, drink, smoke, and wear more, to find room in their groaning bellies for another candy bar....

It cannot last. No society whose values are so warped and tawdry will survive indefinitely. Replete, under-exercised, neurotic, and bored, the *Unpoor* are ill-equipped for the world struggle which has already started.[19]

It appears that man is at present in some kind of limbo; the old has been proved wanting, and rejected, without as yet having been replaced with any declared expression of values with universal acceptance. Somehow, within a potentially explosive situation, the heights and depths of living must be experienced by greater numbers, and the innate power and riches of the human species drawn out of more people; the inherent worth of a life of quality and fulfilment must be demonstrated, in word and deed; and – this above all if man is to *survive* in a way that does not make a mockery of that verb – the unity of the species must become the first article of faith for every world citizen.

It is not inapposite to use the word faith. Michael Novak has written:

> The great leap of faith is faith in man. One must, despite appearances, trust in the power of critical intelligence, courage, and compassion. One must, despite odds, go on struggling for a more brotherly city. Solace between individuals is not enough; community structures must be changed. A reconstruction of the economic, social and political order is called for if men are to develop into men.[20]

Arthur Koestler takes a different approach. Having first developed his thesis that man's greatest danger to himself lies in his proneness to identify himself with a group within society as a whole, with all the inherent dangers of clashing – in matters of principle which at critical moments can lead to violence – with other groups, he describes the existing situation as one in which the human race, divided into so many potentially violent groupings, is playing Russian roulette. He concludes:

> The biological evolution of man seems to have come to a standstill, at least since Cro-Magnon days; since we cannot in the foreseeable future expect a change in human nature to arise by a spontaneous mutation, our only hope seems to be to discover techniques which supplant biological evolution and provide a cure for our collective ailments. Recent ad-

vances in the sciences of life seem to indicate that once man decides to take his fate into his own hands, that possibility will be within his reach.[21]

The question which concerns me is how man is to be persuaded to 'take his fate into his own hands'. There is plenty of evidence of his reluctance to cast himself loose in this way. Many members of the community happily leave to 'them' – whether these be the politicians, local officials, welfare workers or whatever – the responsibilities of the community generally. To be aware brings responsibility which is burdensome enough if it is only oneself of whom one is aware. The burden is inevitably multiplied when the awareness embraces the needs and concerns of the entire human species. How much easier it is to elect a few – the modern replacements for God – to do all the necessary worrying; the danger otherwise may be that of being stifled by one's own humanity!

Perhaps in the end the human race will fail to maintain any faith in itself; perhaps the alleged modern cult of witchcraft and magic is indicative of a basic need – to believe in someone or something other than the human species – which we inherit from our ancestors and will not be denied. My own view is that if these fears prove well-founded, man will have surrendered any right to the titles of power which are so often thrust upon him. If life is only possible in an atmosphere of make-believe, then it is hardly worth living. I for one have spent enough years ridding my system of one myth, without becoming in thrall to another.

I prefer to think that man's reluctance to assume the responsibilities, to seek fulfilment, to embrace some kind of world-view, is brought about by two simple but elemental factors: firstly, he hasn't generally been trained to view life in this way; and secondly, he knows from his own experience that to care for other people may well lead to pain, defeat, and being broken by life. To argue that this is the essence of being human is no consolation to one not prepared since his earliest years for such tribulation: his tendency will be to seek solace in the premature death which is indifference, what Chekhov called the paralysis of the soul. He will not have been able to learn, with William Faulkner, that 'you don't love because; you love despite; not for the virtues, but despite the faults.'

Inheriting the human birthright
How then is man to 'enter into his reward'? How can the values that I have mentioned be appropriated, appreciated, by this

generation, so that men and women, now and in the future, will be motivated by the quest for individual and social fulfilment? If religion can no longer further these values, where can we turn?

Revolution

One school of thought, which may loosely be termed Marxist, affirms that what we seek can be achieved only through political and economic action, which may well involve revolution. Only when society is forcibly brought 'under new management' will the values be able to emerge. If men will not live together; if quantity is not rejected in favour of quality; if people are going to prefer a shallow existence simply because they have never been brought to see the promised land – then this must be imposed on them. How else, it is argued, can you persuade the blind to open their eyes? I recall reading a poem in *Punch* some years ago which began:

> *I spoke of sunrise to a protean newt*
> *That lived in darkness, and had lost his eyes:*
> *He was a creature of a wide repute,*
> *And he replied (and he was very wise):*
> *'There is no sun, therefore it cannot rise.'*

In such a state, it is argued, discussion and debate are useless: you perform a physical operation and *make him see*. This leaves as a moot point the question of how far people can be forced to accept 'what is good for them'. Another issue of *Punch*, years before that poem was published, included a cartoon which depicted a family bank holiday outing. The children all looked intensely miserable, and father, with a savage look on his face, was saying, 'Are you lot going to enjoy yourselves, or am I going to make you?' This suggests that people must first *want* to be humanly rich before they can become so.

However, vociferous groups throughout the world take the other view, and are dedicated to revolution of some kind. If any man still continuing in the Church has adumbrated this attitude in our time, it is Colin Morris. His book *Include Me Out!* reached a wide readership, simply because he expressed himself forcefully as a man who had tried the Church and found its priorities out of order. In *Unyoung, Uncoloured, Unpoor* he pursues this fruitful line of thought. He sees the world's main problems as arising from the fact that most of the power, the riches and the glory rest in the hands of rich old white people. He believes that the inequality of this must be destroyed, and rejects

142

any concept of gentle persuasion, passive resistance, or anything short of violence in order to achieve it. The bomb and the sword are, he feels, regrettably the only means left to the three categories of people summarized in the title by which to achieve their freedom, their basic human rights. He points out that Bonhoeffer, hailed in so many circles as the prophet of our age, was executed – justly – for his part in a plot to assassinate the nation's leader. He suggests that unless Christians accept this method of persuasion, either the existing rulers will continue to rule, or Christians will be outflanked, in providing an alternative, by anarchists, Marxists, the Black Power movement, the 'new left' or any other of the numerous revolutionary movements which have emerged in the past decade.

He writes:

> There is much smashing down as well as building up to be done in our generation, and lack of a stomach for wielding the sledge-hammer could consign Christians to the spectators' enclosure whilst Marxists, anarchists, and Black Power advocates do the brutal work necessary to break a way into the future.

He has no time for the wider perspective afforded by the concept of a world beyond this, where injustices will be rectified:

> Pious talk of awaiting a Kingdom beyond history comes easily to the warm and well-fed. They won't find the delay too arduous. But in the brute battle for survival, every day is an eternity. Who can blame the down-trodden for feeling they must act now, and damn the consequences?[22]

In one section of the book he gives a portrayal of Jesus as – far from the 'meek and mild' picture of Victorian times – a revolutionary who was executed for encouraging rebellion against the Roman state. I have a good deal of sympathy with this picture, if only because it is of a human Jesus, committed to the historical process, a man amongst men. Morris's references in support of his thesis on this point are too numerous to be summarized here, and I refer the reader to chapter six of his book.

Morris is a rare bird in ecclesiastical circles (and I'm bound to add that I find his position in a highly traditional ecclesiastical situation somewhat anomalous in the light of his revolutionary discourses) and one wonders how long it will be before he becomes a professional politician. Certainly he has captured a current mood; but for all his tough talk, it is to the secular revolutionaries that we must look if we are to understand the strategy and tactics of change – to those who feel no need to justify their actions from the life of Jesus, or from anything other than the needs presented by the contemporary situation. For those who believe in a policy of violence, Marcuse, probably more than anyone else, symbolizes the attitude required: 'be a detonator.' Among students throughout the world, in France, Germany, Italy and Great Britain, in America and Japan, these words have sparked off a foment, the end of which cannot be foreseen. The campus revolt, the 'new left', Black Power: all these movements hold the key to the peacefulness or otherwise of the next twenty years.

It is tempting at this point to enter into a lengthy discourse analysing revolutions which have been beneficial, and detrimental to the human species throughout history. The conclusions that would be reached, however, would have little relevance to the present situation, since I believe that each situation must be judged pragmatically, and that therefore nothing can be learned from history: the present situation must be judged on present understanding. Instead, I prefer to state why, although I may well agree with the analysis of society made at some point by Marxists, student power movements, and so on, I consider their actions to be only dealing with the surface, so far as human values are concerned.

My view is that, if or when these movements rectify any injustices which they were motivated to deal with, the problem of finding human values will remain. We may argue with the Marxists that Jack is as good as his master, and establish a system where this is seen to be so; but if Jack then turns on his former masters and treats them as less than human, little progress will have been made. Though tactically useful at times, revolution is irrelevant as strategy.[23] In the short term it may overcome any aspects of a system which blatantly smother human values among a specific section of the population. But whether, following a revolution, these values will be allowed to emerge and be given free expression in the lives of the entire population is a matter totally independent of the revolution. Those who believe that paradise is just around the corner, with only one more political upheaval required, have always been the short-sighted ones. What is required now is for the total commitment of the revolutionaries to the human situation – undiluted secularity, if you like – combined with a deeper view of human nature.

Education

The only major area of life where this problem can be tackled exhaustively is *education*. The Plowden report, *Children and Their Primary Schools*, acknowledges this when, in words which I find admirable in their clarity, it states:

> A school is not merely a teaching shop, it must transmit values and attitudes. It is a community in which children learn to live first and foremost as children and not as future adults. In family life children learn to live with people of all ages. The school sets out deliberately to devise the right environment for children, to allow them to be themselves and to develop in the way and at the pace appropriate to them. It tries to equalise opportunities and to compensate for handicaps. It lays special stress on individual discovery, on first hand experience and on opportunities for creative work. It insists that knowledge does not fall into neatly separate compartments and that work and play are not opposite but complementary. A child brought up in such an atmosphere at all stages of his education has some hope of becoming a balanced and mature adult and of being able to live in, to contribute to, and to look critically at, the society of which he forms a part. Not all primary schools correspond to this picture, but it does represent a general and quickening trend.[24]

This statement goes a long way towards defining the aims in terms which enunciate the outlook presented in this book. It recognizes what is required at a much deeper level than do many of the sociologists writing about education. Havighurst and Neugarten affirm for instance:

> In a democratic society the school system is called upon to work toward two somewhat different goals: one, of improving society and promoting social change; the other, of stabilizing society and preserving the status quo.[25]

It could be acknowledged that on the wider questions of education – exemplified in the comprehensive versus three-tier system – this is the case; I find this inadequate as a description of what happens at the operational level – in the classroom or lecture room, face to face with pupils or students. There, the issue is a more personal one: how shall these young people best be equipped to tackle the great issues of living, along the lines outlined in the quotation from Plowden. Whether, once equipped, they go out to promote social change or to stabilize society will depend on their own individual assessments of the situation, and on the particular social issues which eventually confront them. What I am more concerned about is the values which they hold, and the strength with which they will desire to maintain them.

The social reconstructionist attitude to education is more relevant in the developing countries, as there is more obvious need for it. Various educational reports of African governments – in particular, that for Tanzania – evince this approach. The most explicit statement along these lines that I have yet read is the Government of India's Report of the Education Commission (1964–66) 'Education and National Development'. This report defines development as an injection into the ancient (and valid) culture, with its overlay of the more recent (and invalid) imperialist culture, of 'modernization' – in industry, agriculture, and scientific and technological thinking. Indian education has been geared to meet the vocational and administrative needs of a feudal, imperial society, educationally strongly influenced by the English public school system. The imperial tie has been broken, but the educational mentality lingers on; therefore a new approach to education is required since it alone can feed the socio-cultural revolution which the authors of the report foresee. They state explicitly:

> If this 'change on a grand scale' is to be achieved without violent revolution (and even then it would still be necessary) there is one instrument, and one instrument only, that can be used: EDUCATION. Other agencies may help, and can indeed sometimes have a more apparent impact. But the national system of education is the only instrument that can reach all the people.[26]

The authors then suggest how education could be the catalyst of change in each of the areas under consideration – and how it could encourage modernization, geared to human resource developments, disseminated throughout the country. They add:

> In a democracy, the individual is an end in himself, and the primary purpose of education is to provide him with the widest opportunity to develp his potentialities to the full. But the path to this goal lies through social reorganisation and emphasis on social perspectives. . . . Individual fulfilment will come, not through selfish and narrow loyalties to personal or group interests, but through the dedication of all to the wider loyalties of national development in all its parameters.

Some may criticize this last statement because it seems to advocate propaganda rather than education; but we must recognize the tremendous pressures facing anyone concerned with dragging India into the 20th century without suffering an upheaval so wide-spread that contemporary society would disappear altogether. The important point for our discussion is that in a national situation vastly different from the British, it is recognized, as in the Plowden Report, that education is the main area in which the seeds of personal and social fulfilment may be sown. And this would remain just as true, even if there is a Marxist or any other kind of revolution. It confirms my point that revolution is a short-term process which may produce conditions more conducive to the human values I should like to see accepted universally, but will do nothing, either to individuals or communities, to inculcate these values. Revolution may be necessary in order to cut out the rotten wood: the main job will still remain.

Can we then – and we think now specifically of the situation in the British Isles – leave it to the sphere of education to disseminate human values? Has education taken over from religion? There are reasons why only a half- (or quarter-) hearted affirmative can be given to this. Firstly, although those involved in education may do their best to withstand this, the pressures of society cannot ultimately be overcome. And unfortunately for those concerned with values, many of these pressures bespeak attitudes which can be described only as materialistic. Because qualifications are at a premium, the worth of a subject to be studied is judged by many according to its relative worth in the examination at the end of the course. 'You'd better learn this: it's a favourite with the examiners' is a remark which is the antithesis of education; yet few students pursue their courses without having such statements frequently thrown at them. The idea of a piece of writing as an end itself, of an area of enquiry being studied purely for the sake of understanding better the world men inhabit, of examining a proposition critically so that, if found wanting, it may be discarded: all these have little place in a society which at almost every level demands paper qualifications indicating competence in a field, rather than the power to analyse, catalyse, or create.

At the earliest stages, in primary schools, it is possible for teachers and children to work more independently of society's demands; there, at least, work is not judged solely by the amount it pays. But this raises the second problem: are the teachers themselves – who are, after all, products of the society whose attitudes have been criticized – 'big' enough to overcome the pressures and concentrate on the main aims of education as Plowden describes them? One of the correspondents on my *Guardian* article 'Bringing Down the Mighty' stated:

> I have a humble and humiliating job as a primary school headmaster, comparable in affliction, I suppose, to that of many parsons. The humiliation is derived, I think, from reluctantly compromising with a system occupied and motivated in the main by people who overtly avow and support the idea that education should enable us to use to the full our innate powers and sentience, but who in practice condone and encourage subservience to the immediate interests of established structures.

Of course, in their training they may receive suggestions about creative teaching: the question is how long they are able to withstand the ingrained conservatism of many of the 'old dogs' they encounter in the average staff-room. (In any case, this begs the question of the attitudes of the teacher trainers. Perhaps we need in this country something along the lines of the three T's experiment in Harvard – training the trainers of teachers – but then one would have to have great confidence in those operating the course.) My own experience of the teaching profession suggests that, while a minority are aware of the great human issues of our time and see their own work in the light of this, the great majority are simply earning their living conscientiously, and cannot be looked to for anything more profound than competently completing the syllabus, or their own schemes of work.

The third problem relates to the home background of the children. Although no teacher should allow such considerations to deter him from making the attempt to educate in its fullest sense, many recognize that some children are stunted from the start by what their parents have done to them during the crucial first five years of their lives. Compulsory nursery school attendance from the age of three, or even two, may help to alleviate the harm done by such parents, but it is a problem which will not be overcome until the state generally – to whom, rather than to the parents, the children ultimately 'belong' – makes parentcraft a compulsory course for all, either at school or during the engagement period. It seems to me strange that men and women can become parents, having the power to maim their children psychologically for life, yet they are virtually untouchable. In fact, considering the harm done even by so many socially acceptable parents who are yet

148

more interested in themselves than in their children, I feel that the time has come to ask how long the family can continue to be the basic structure of society. Do we need something more reliable for the rearing of children in the community than the present hit-or-miss process?

All this is raising weighty matters which cannot be pursued further in this book. My conclusion is that, while education is the one sphere in which values can be inculcated, the attitudes of society militate against the extensive dissemination of these values which is essential if education is to be worthy of the name – drawing out, rather than putting in.

What, then, are we left with? Do we surrender and fall back on despair that the human race will progress towards maturity according to its birthright? Or is there perhaps a certain naturalism about the process? Certainly when one considers the writings of Galbraith, Leach, Anatol Rapopot, contributors to 'New Society's World in 1984' series, speakers at the 1967 Pugwash and World Mental Health Congresses, it is clear that men's minds generally are beginning to awaken to the possibilities within the present situation.

It may well be that we are forced back to Plato's conception of the small group of élite who provide the ideas which motivate the rest of society. Provided such an élite has ideas in accordance with my own, it is not painful to contemplate this! The correspondent just quoted outlined the individual members of such an élite who had influenced him:

> I find acceptable notions of reality in GBS (the life force driving one's wits), in Samuel Beckett (the ludicrous search for individuality and identity, when equipped only with a carcase subject to decrepitude – the pitiful search for somewhere to stay, and be at rest), in Ecclesiastes and its worldliness, in several novels, plays, poems, and in many of the sciences; but most of all, perhaps, in human genius, the essence of an individual persisting beyond the circumscriptions and overcoming.

My own list would include Arthur Koestler and his concern for a unified world community; Julian Huxley with his vision of world and individual fulfilment; Bertrand Russell with his crystal-clear assessment of the potentialities for both glory and destruction facing the human species; Albert Camus and his concept of resurrection as the moment when, because one is no longer alienated from oneself, one is not alienated from one's fellows; and the visionary Teilhard de Chardin, with his concept of man in the evolutionary process. These, together with some of those named above, and other writers – and, occasionally, film-producers – seem to me to be the élite who are directing the energies of our age so that men are encouraged to rise above the petty materialism, narrowness of vision, paucity of relationships, which would deprive them of their destiny.

Whether there is time for their ideas to seminate before either a nuclear holocaust, global racial war, world economic collapse, death through atmospheric poisoning, suffocation through overcrowding, or the natural death of the solar system cannot be judged. As a natural optimist I maintain my faith in man, despite the hundred-and-one reasons constantly presented to me to abandon this. It seems reasonable to believe that among the 3000 million of us there is enough intelligence, energy, will-power to use the natural forces which constitute our environment – biological, chemical, psychological – for man's wellbeing. I am downcast by the way society tries to strait-jacket its members, in terms of the work they do, the way they live, the ideas they hold. Man is idiosyncratic, not made to be fodder for mass political and economic planning. It is for him, therefore, to create environments in which he can survive to fulfil himself; and this needs above all the assurance that each individual *matters*. As my correspondent wrote,

> The barriers are profits, markets, commercialism, class, race, nationalism, ideologies, prejudices, cultures, beliefs, customs, ignorance, complacency, hypocrisy, and all the forces that inhibit open thinking.

In other words, we need 'man-without-labels'; man mature enough not to need the crutch of any limited association in order to be able to look the world in the face; man who recognizes at the same time both his oneness with all others and his distinctiveness from them; man who, while realizing that he is dust and ashes, yet recognizes the other side of the paradox that for his sake the universe was made – a teleological position which may ultimately be disproved but which seems reasonable at the present stage of the evolutionary process.

In the final paragraph of his book *Has Man a Future?* Bertrand Russell paints a picture of man-as-he-might-be. Some would condemn this as impossibly idealistic and romantic; I believe that his picture, granted the premises, is a fair one – and one which the human species needs to have constantly before the eyes. Having argued that man no longer needs a dream of Heaven in order to give him something to which to look forward; and, after suggesting that through education the 'undigested science' of our age could be assimilated, he states:

> If our present troubles can be conquered, Man can look forward to a future immeasurably longer than his past, inspired by a new breadth of vision, a continuing hope perpetually fed by a continuing achievement. Man has made a beginning creditable for an infant – for, in a biological sense, Man, the latest of the species, is still an infant. No limit can be set to what he may achieve in the future. I see, in my mind's eye, a world of glory and joy, a world where minds expand, where hope remains undimmed, and what is noble is no longer condemned as treachery to this or that paltry aim. All this can happen if we will let it happen. It rests with our generation to decide between this vision and an end decreed by folly.

The greatest human value is man himself. If the implications of this can be appreciated, then perhaps we shall see an end to the cynicism, the despair, the shallowness too frequently experienced in human life today; and perhaps generations centuries hence will look back on our age as both a continuation of the Dark Ages, and the herald of the dawn when the glimmer of twilight first seen at the time of the Renaissance became the radiance of the full light of day.

POSTCRIPT

THE strength of *Honest to God*, I have been told, lay in three factors: one, John Robinson was a Bishop when he wrote it; two, he remained a Bishop afterwards; three, he showed that 'his heart was in the right place' – he was still, physically and psychologically, part of the Church.

I wish to make no invidious comparisons between the present volume and *Honest to God* so far as intellectual profundity is concerned. Dr. Robinson is a scholar; I am not. Yet, so far as the natural direction of thought is concerned, I believe that what I have said represents a logical further step, hinted at in Robinson's foreword.[1]

In 1964, the Church ceased to be the physical focal-point of my life, even though I was officially a member of the St. Mary's staff. For some time the needle moved backwards and forwards, until it finally rested on Further Education: there, at any rate until the present, it has remained. Since then – and writing this book has impressed this on me – I have ceased to find the Church a psychological focal-point, as it had continued to be for some time after I was no longer a circuit minister. Although I remain nominally a Methodist minister, I am an outsider – a Christian outsider, on the broadest definition of that word; but the key word is outsider. I find that I cannot tolerate church services: ancient or modern, they bore and exasperate me. So I no longer attend church except when invited to speak at a service. Equally, I find no help in my quest from theological writings – ancient or modern; they fill me with the sense that, however progressive their authors may consider themselves to be, they reflect thought-forms and concepts which are dead – and which ought to be buried. So I no longer read theological books, except when compelled to do so by specific duties, like writing this book.

To many (and I know that this is said) I have simply become a humanist, and ought therefore to resign from the ministry. To the first charge I will reply in some words which I wrote in a *Times* article, 'Breaking the barriers of an argument without end':

The supreme need for man today is to (think for himself).

153

He needs to work out his own salvation and discover an expression of the meaning and purpose of life in human terms.

In this quest, the Christian culture has a positive, valuable, and unique part to play. The Christian gospel teaches fulfilment through abundant living; it understands that life can be a heaven or hell according to one's ability to live alongside other people in an attitude of goodwill and tolerance. It recognizes the great secret, which humanists and secularists often seem either unable or unwilling to acknowledge, that love and suffering (in the sense of sympathy) go hand-in-hand; and in the myth of the resurrection is embodied the truth that when man comes to terms with himself there is in his life a joy, a direction and a purpose which may otherwise be missed.

I reject any charge, therefore, of having switched camps. Indeed, I refuse to recognize the need for the continuance of any camps. Man is indivisible, and the need is for all men of compassion, courage and insight to come together in order to ensure that man's future on this planet remains hopeful.

The Christian need not fear that what he has dedicated himself to will thereby be invalidated. Rather he should learn that only in this way can the basic human values and insights embodied in the Christian gospel be recovered for this and any future generation, instead of atrophying within a discarded myth.[2]

To accuse me of being a humanist, therefore, is not to recognize my attempt to take the argument on to totally new ground (or perhaps is an indication of the feebleness of my attempt.) There are enough people inside and outside the church concerned about the kind of issues raised in the last part of section four – and concerned deeply enough – to obviate the need for any theological vindication of what is done. Let those who are theologians first and human beings second remain in their churches; and let those secularists who wish to spend their energies denying the validity of Christian claims, toppling the Christian Establishment, and twisting biblical students into knots, continue to do so. Neither of these types has a place in the present debate, as neither can survive into the future except as warnings to others of culs-de-sac ahead. For myself, if to be religious is to be profoundly concerned about the human condition and human destiny, about meaning and purpose in life, about the relationship of man to man –

then I submit that I am intensely religious. My argument is that the word lends itself to so many interpretations – some of them mutually exclusive – that I prefer to let it drop, and be known simply as one who is profoundly concerned about the human condition.

The second point follows from this. If I am logical, it is argued, I will cease functioning, even in the small way I do now, within any Christian congregation. By my own confession I no longer believe the Christian doctrines as traditionally preached: how, then, can I continue to appear before any congregation which assembles with the expectancy of hearing 'the Word of God' proclaimed?

To suggest this is to beg the whole question I am raising: how important are the Church's doctrines as doctrines? How many worshippers attend services to have their theology straightened out, and how many because they, like me, are deeply concerned about the human issues facing them? To take one example: how necessary is it, for an understanding of what Camus called 'resurrection' in the lives of human beings, to accept literally the story of the resurrection as recounted in the Gospels? Is not the point of the narrative the effect on the disciples? And is not this the sole point of contact between those narratives and present-day congregations, or communities anywhere? My own conviction is that, in demythologizing the Gospel, I am helping to make clear the essential message which was in the mind of Jesus and the evangelists in the first place. I believe this message to be intensely human, to which everything that we loosely term 'the supernatural' is irrelevant, if not deterrent. I therefore view myself as one who is attempting, in a small way, to rescue churchgoers from their own past. I realize that this sounds presumptuous and pompous, but how else can any preacher justify the fact that congregations sit and listen to what he has to expound?

My aim, then, is to play a positive role in the current debate. If I were to withdraw altogether from church life, I should be viewed simply as one who had 'lost his faith' and gone over to the 'other side'. Willy-nilly, I should be pigeon-holed; and it is precisely *this* that I refuse to be.

If I haven't been entirely logical (and who can be logical all the time? – there is the fact of one's roots, one's friends, to be taken into consideration) at least I hope this has clarified the situation in which I find myself. If the viewpoint proposed in this book be accepted, the question of 'camps' should never be introduced. I am if you like, a Christian atheist, an agnostic believer, a religious humanist, a faithful heretic, a schismless iconoclast, a pagan theologian, an orthodox apostate, a sceptical dogmatist, a polytheistic monotheist. If that doesn't render the discussion absurd, I'll follow the advice of one of my sons, and spend the rest of my life minding a hole in the road. The title of this book gives as clear an indication as any of my position. But my prime wish is to be known only as a member of the human race, deeply concerned about the human situation. As Michael Lane, one of the non-church supporters, stated in a *Guardian* article:

> Maybe we must have movements and parties and labels. . . . but surely we must recognize that none of these movements should be accorded overriding importance, that no commitment, except that so general as to be platitudinous – a commitment to life and humanity itself – is all-embracing. All loyalties must be judged in the light of our allegiance to the whole world of experience and to the human race without distinction.[3]

Within this general context, I hope there is still a place for the explorer. Perhaps, like most physical explorers, I can never feel really at home in the known, established, secure world which is most people's environment. Perhaps in terms of a philosophy of life I shall always be an outsider to any currently accepted view. This may not be very helpful to anyone else, but it satisfies me. Some words which have haunted me all my life are the final paragraph of Apsley Cherry-Garrard's *The Worst Journey in the World*. Translated into the world of ideas, they speak to my condition; and perhaps occasionally what is discovered is helpful for those more settled in familiar surroundings:

> And I tell you, if you have the desire for knowledge and the power to give it physical expression, go out and explore. If you are a brave man you will do nothing; if you are fearful, you may do much, for none but cowards have need to prove their bravery. Some will tell you that you are mad, and nearly all will say: 'What is the use?' For we are a nation of shopkeepers, and no shopkeeper will look at research which does not promise him a financial return within a year. And so you will sledge nearly alone, but those with whom you sledge will not be shopkeepers; that is worth a good deal. If you march your Winter Journeys you will have your reward, so long as all you want is a penguin's egg.

REFERENCES

Section One

No. Page

1   29   *About the Ministry*, Epworth, 1967, p. 68.

2   31   *The Pioneer Ministry*, p. 72. Quoted in Stacey, op. cit., p. 44.

3   31   Stacey, op. cit., pp. 48f.

4   33   *New Christian*, 16 June 1966.

5   33   *Educational Explorers*, 1967.

6   34   Cf. K. Grayston's report on a WCC conference on this theme, *New Christian*, 10 August 1967.

7   35   G. Winter, *The New Creation as Metropolis*, Macmillan, New York, 1963, pp. 93f.

8   36   *New Christian*, 16 June 1966.

9   36   Many ministers forget that they can add little short of £1,000 p.a. to their stipends for the rent-free, rates-free houses which they enjoy, and don't even have to pay to maintain. Add to this (a) the amount of tax that they would have paid to earn rents/mortgage and rates; (b) the fees for weddings, etc.; (c) the part-time teaching, etc., which many perform – and few will have a real income lower than £2,500 p.a. And some still grumble about the small-ness of their car allowances!

10   37   Prof. Harry Ree, *Guardian*, 6 January 1970.

11   37   Isaiah 43:12.

12   38   *The Myth of Sisyphus*.

13   39   June 1966.

14   40   *Presbyterian Messenger*, November 1966.

Section Two

1   43   Cf. C. Michalson, *Japanese Contributions to Christian Theology*, Westminster Press, Philadelphia, pp. 18ff.

2   50   See Section Three for further discussion of 'political theology'.

3   53   Reprinted from *Objections to Humanism*, Constable, 1965, pp. 26f.

4   54   Op. cit., April 1965.

5   55   *New Christian*, 12 January 1967.

6   56   *New Christian*, 21 March 1968.

7   57   1965–66.

8   58   Op. cit., 26 March 1963.

No.	Page	
9	59	*The Noise of Solemn Assemblies*, Doubleday, New York, 1961, p. 152.
10	59	*New Christian*, 26 January 1967.
11	59	Holt, Rinehart and Winston, New York, 1967.
12	64	*The New Reformation?*, SCM, 1963, ch. 4.
13	64	Cf. Julian Huxley, *The Crisis in Man's Destiny*, *Playboy*, January 1967.
14	64	*New Christian*, 25 August 1965.
15	65	Op. cit.
16	65	*The Old Reformation and the New*, Epworth, 1967, p. 51.
17	68	*The Noise of Solemn Assemblies*, p. 170.

Section Three

1	83	October 1966, Ed. R. J. Billington.
2	85	*Playboy*, December 1965.
3	86	*Das Wesen des Christentums*, 1841. Eng. trans. George Eliot, 1853.
4	87	*A Common Faith*, pp. 42f, 50.
5	88	*Honest to God*, SCM, 1963, pp. 50f.
6	90	*Playboy*, December 1965, cf. Altizer, *The Gospel of Christian Atheism*, Westminster, N.Y., 1966.
7	94	*Objections to Humanism*, pp. 50f.
8	95	*The Myth of Sisyphus*.
9	100	R. G. Jones and A. J. Wesson, *Towards a Radical Church*, Epworth, 1970.
10	101	Op. cit.
11	101	*Guardian*, Whit Saturday 1967.
12	102	*The Secular Meaning of the Gospel*, SCM, 1963, p. 120.
13	102	*The New Testament in Current Study*, SCM, 1963.
14	103	Cf. Matt. 23.
15	105	1 Cor. 15.
16	105	Op. cit., p. 129.
17	108	Luke 4:16.
18	109	John 4.
19	109	John 14:9; 10:30.
20	111	Collins, 1969.
21	111	Epworth, 1970.
22	111	Op. cit., p. 170.
23	112	P. 74
24	112	Reputedly the wealthiest suburb in New York.
25	113	Op. cit., p. 49.
26	114	Op. cit., pp. 137f.
27	115	*The Secular City*, SCM, 1965, pp. 18–21.
28	115	*Christianity and Crisis*, December 1966, pp. 294–7. Quoted

No. Page

in McBrien, op. cit., pp. 26f.

29   115   Op. cit., p. 21.
30   116   *Christ in a Nuclear World*, Crux Press, 1962, pp. 159f.
31   117   SCM, 1968.
32   117   *Playboy*, January 1967.
33   118   February 1967.
34   119   Statement by the Californian Migrant Ministry, 14 December 1965.
35   119   *Over the Bridge*, April 1965.
36   120   *On Not Leaving it to the Snake*, SCM, 1968, p. 143.

Section Four
1   123   Herder and Herder, 1969, pp. 17f.
2   124   Article 'The New Divinity' in *Twentieth Century*.
3   125   Op. cit., p. 37.
4   127   *The Secular City*, ch. 2.
5   127   *Evening News*, London, 29 July 1967.
6   129   If Matt. 5; 32b, be quoted against this, it must be replied that this is the Gospel written with Jewish readers in mind, as 5:18 indicates; and that if the Church is going to treat the comment on divorce as an absolute injunction, what line should be taken on 19:21?
7   132   Wilson, Williams, Sugarman, *Introduction to Moral Education*, Penguin, 1967, p. 301.
8   132   Op. cit., p. 307.
9   133   Op. cit., p. 109.
10   133   Do. p. 111.
11   134   *Has Man a Future?* Penguin, 1961, pp. 126f.
12   136   Op. cit., p. 41.
13   137   *Britain in the Sixties: The Family and Marriage*, Penguin, 1962.
14   137   *Playboy*, January 1967.
15   137   *Uses of Literacy*, Penguin, 1957.
16   138   *Rain Upon Godshill*.
17   138   *Help*, No. 11.
18   138   Jonathan Cape, 1969.
19   140   *Unyoung, Uncoloured, Unpoor*, Epworth, 1969, pp. 78f.
20   140   Op. cit., p. 106.
21   141   *Observer*, 28 April 1968.
22   143   Op. cit., pp. 25, 98.
23   144   One example where violent action (anomalously enough, counter-revolutionary in the circumstances) would have been justified was when Ian Smith made his UDI. Had the British troops walked in, taken over all government build-

No. Page

ings, imprisoned the cabinet, and brought blacks into the
government, we might have been accused of violence, but
hardly of immorality.

24   145   Ch. 15, para. 505.
25   145   *Society and Education*, Allyn and Bacon, 1967.
26   146   Op. cit., ch. 1, para. 14.

Postscript
1   153   *Honest to God*, pp. 9f.
2   154   1 March 1969.
3   156   September 1968.